# COBRAS
# & Replicas
# 1962-1983

Compiled by
R.M. Clarke

ISBN 0 946 489 181

Distributed by
Brooklands Book Distribution Ltd.
'Holmerise', Seven Hills Road,
Cobham, Surrey, England

## BROOKLANDS BOOKS SERIES

AC Ace & Aceca 1953-1983
AC Cobra 1962-1969
Alfa Romeo Giulia Coupés 1963-1976
Alfa Romeo Spider 1966-1981
Austin Seven 1922-1982
Austin A30 & A35 1951-1962
Austin Healey 100 1952-1959
Austin Healey 3000 1959-1967
Austin Healey 100 & 3000 Collection No. 1
Austin Healey 'Frogeye' Sprite Collection No. 1
Austin Healey Sprite 1958-1971
Avanti 1962-1983
BMW Six Cylinder Coupés 1969-1975
BMW 1600 Collection No. 1
BMW 2002 Collection No. 1
Buick Riviera 1963-1978
Cadillac Eldorado 1967-1978
Cadillac in the Sixties No. 1
Camaro 1966-1970
Chevrolet Camaro Collection No. 1
Chevelle & SS 1964-1972
Chevy II Nova & SS 1962-1973
Chrysler 300 1955-1970
Citroen Traction Avant 1934-1957
Citroen 2CV 1949-1982
Cobras & Replicas 1969-1983
Cortina 1600E & GT 1967-1970
Corvair 1959-1968
Daimler Dart & V-8 250 1959-1969
Datsun 240z & 260z 1970-1977
De Tomaso Collection No. 1
Dodge Charger 1966-1974
Excalibur Collection No. 1
Ferrari Cars 1946-1956
Ferrari Cars 1962-1966
Ferrari Cars 1966-1969
Ferrari Cars 1969-1973
Ferrari Dino 1965-1974
Ferrari Dino 308 1974-1979
Ferrari 308 & Mondial 1980-1984
Ferrari Collection No. 1
Fiat X1/9 1972-1980
Ford GT40 1964-1978
Ford Mustang 1964-1967
Ford Mustang 1967-1973
Ford RS Escort 1968-1980
High Performance Escorts MkI 1968-1974
High Performance Escorts MkII 1975-1980
Hudson & Railton Cars 1936-1940
Jaguar (& S.S) Cars 1931-1937
Jaguar Cars 1948-1951
Jaguar Cars 1957-1961
Jaguar Cars 1961-1964
Jaguar Cars 1964-1968
Jaguar E-Type 1961-1966
Jaguar E-Type 1966-1971
Jaguar E-Type 1971-1975
Jaguar XKE Collection No. 1
Jaguar XJ6 1968-1972
Jaguar XJ6 Series II 1973-1979
Jaguar XJ6 & XJ12 Series III 1979-1985
Jaguar XJ12 1972-1980
Jaguar XJS 1975-1980
Jensen Cars 1946-1967
Jensen Cars 1967-1979
Jensen Interceptor 1966-1976
Jensen-Healey 1972-1976
Lamborghini Cars 1964-1970
Lamborghini Cars 1970-1975
Lamborghini Countach Collection No. 1
Lamborghini Countach & Urraco 1974-1980
Lamborghini Countach & Jalpa 1980-1985
Lancia Stratos 1972-1985
Land Rover 1948-1973
Land Rover 1958-1983
Lotus Cortina 1963-1970
Lotus Elan 1962-1973
Lotus Elan Collection No. 1
Lotus Elan Collection No. 2
Lotus Elite 1957-1964
Lotus Elite & Eclat 1974-1981
Lotus Esprit 1974-1981
Lotus Europa 1966-1975
Lotus Europa Collection No. 1
Lotus Seven 1957-1980
Lotus Seven Collection No. 1
Maserati 1965-1970
Maserati 1970-1975
Mazda RX-7 Collection No. 1
Mercedes 230/250/280SL 1963-1971
Mercedes 350/450SL & SLC 1971-1980
Mercedes Benz Cars 1949-1954
Mercedes Benz Cars 1954-1957
Mercedes Benz Cars 1957-1961
Mercedes Benz Competition Cars 1950-1957

Metropolitan 1954-1962
MG Cars 1929-1934
MG Cars 1935-1940
MG TC 1945-1949
MG TD 1949-1953
MG TF 1953-1955
MG Cars 1957-1959
MG Cars 1959-1962
MG Midget 1961-1980
MG MGA 1955-1962
MGA Collection No. 1
MG MGB 1962-1970
MG MGB 1970-1980
MGB GT 1965-1980
Mini Cooper 1961-1971
Morgan Cars 1960-1970
Morgan Cars 1969-1979
Morris Minor Collection No. 1
Old's Cutlass & 4-4-2 1964-1972
Oldsmobile Toronado 1966-1978
Opel GT 1968-1973
Pantera 1970-1973
Pantera & Mangusta 1969-1974
Plymouth Barracuda 1964-1974
Pontiac GTO 1964-1970
Pontiac Firebird 1967-1973
Pontiac Tempest & GTO 1961-1965
Porsche Cars 1960-1964
Porsche Cars 1964-1968
Porsche Cars 1968-1972
Porsche Cars in the Sixties
Porsche Cars 1972-1975
Porsche 356 1952-1965
Porsche 911 Collection No. 1
Porsche 911 Collection No. 2
Porsche 911 1965-1969
Porsche 911 1970-1972
Porsche 911 1973-1977
Porsche 911 Carrera 1973-1977
Porsche 911 SC 1978-1983
Porsche 911 Turbo 1975-1984
Porsche 914 1969-1975
Porsche 914 Collection No. 1
Porsche 924 1975-1981
Porsche 928 Collection No. 1
Porsche 944 1981-1985
Porsche Turbo Collection No. 1
Reliant Scimitar 1964-1982
Rolls Royce Silver Cloud 1955-1965
Rolls Royce Silver Shadow 1965-1980
Range Rover 1970-1981
Rover 3 & 3.5 Litre 1958-1973
Rover P4 1949-1959
Rover P4 1955-1964
Rover 2000 + 2200 1963-1977
Saab Sonett Collection No. 1
Saab Turbo 1976-1983
Singer Sports Cars 1933-1934
Studebaker Hawks & Larks 1956-1963
Sunbeam Alpine & Tiger 1959-1967
Thunderbird 1955-1957
Thunderbird 1958-1963
Triumph 2000-2.5-2500 1963-1977
Triumph Spitfire 1962-1980
Triumph Spitfire Collection No. 1
Triumph Stag 1970-1980
Triumph Stag Collection No. 1
Triumph TR2 & TR3 1952-1960
Triumph TR4.TR5.TR250 1961-1968
Triumph TR6 Collection No. 1
Triumph TR7 & TR8 1975-1981
Triumph GT6 1966-1974
Triumph Vitesse & Herald 1959-1971
TVR 1960-1980
Volkswagen Cars 1936-1956
VW Beetle 1956-1979
VW Beetle Collection No. 1
VW Karmann Ghia 1955-1982
VW Scirocco 1974-1981
Volvo 1800 1960-1973
Volvo 120 Series 1956-1970

## BROOKLANDS MUSCLE CARS SERIES

American Motor Muscle Cars 1966-1970
Buick Muscle Cars 1965-1970
Camaro Muscle Cars 1966-1972
Capri Muscle Cars 1969-1983
Chevrolet Muscle Cars 1966-1972
Dodge Muscle Cars 1967-1979
Mercury Muscle Cars 1966-1971
Mini Muscle Cars 1961-1979
Mopar Muscle Cars 1964-1967
Mopar Muscle Cars 1968-1971
Mustang Muscle Cars 1967-1971
Shelby Mustang Muscle Cars 1965-1970
Oldsmobile Muscle Cars 1964-1970

Plymouth Muscle Cars 1966-1971
Pontiac Muscle Cars 1966-1972
Muscle Cars Compared 1966-1971
Muscle Cars Compared Book 2 1965-1971

## BROOKLANDS ROAD & TRACK SERIES

Road & Track on Alfa Romeo 1949-1963
Road & Track on Alfa Romeo 1964-1970
Road & Track on Alfa Romeo 1971-1976
Road & Track on Alfa Romeo 1977-1984
Road & Track on Aston Martin 1962-1984
Road & Track on Austin Healey 1953-1970
Road & Track on BMW Cars 1966-1974
Road & Track on BMW Cars 1975-1978
Road & Track on BMW Cars 1979-1983
Road & Track on Cobra, Shelby &
Ford GT40 1962-1983
Road & Track on Corvette 1953-1967
Road & Track on Corvette 1968-1982
Road & Track on Datsun Z 1970-1983
Road & Track on Ferrari 1950-1968
Road & Track on Ferrari 1968-1974
Road & Track on Ferrari 1975-1981
Road & Track on Ferrari 1981-1984
Road & Track on Fiat Sports Cars 1968-1981
Road & Track on Jaguar 1950-1960
Road & Track on Jaguar 1961-1968
Road & Track on Jaguar 1968-1974
Road & Track on Jaguar 1974-1982
Road & Track on Lamborghini 1964-1982
Road & Track on Lotus 1972-1981
Road & Track on Maserati 1952-1974
Road & Track on Maserati 1975-1983
Road & Track on Mercedes Sports & GT Cars
1970-1980
Road & Track on MG Sports Cars 1949-1961
Road & Track on MG Sports Cars 1962-1980
Road & Track on Pontiac 1960-1983
Road & Track on Porsche 1951-1967
Road & Track on Porsche 1968-1971
Road & Track on Porsche 1972-1975
Road & Track on Porsche 1975-1978
Road & Track on Porsche 1979-1982
Road & Track on Porsche 1982-1985
Road & Track on Rolls Royce & Bentley 1950-1965
Road & Track on Rolls Royce & Bentley 1966-1984
Road & Track on Saab 1955-1985
Road & Track on Triumph Sports Cars 1953-1967
Road & Track on Triumph Sports Cars 1967-1974
Road & Track on Triumph Sports Cars 1974-1982
Road & Track on Volkswagen 1951-1968
Road & Track on Volkswagen 1968-1978
Road & Track on Volkswagen 1978-1985
Road & Track on Volvo 1957-1974
Road & Track on Volvo 1975-1985

## BROOKLANDS CAR AND DRIVER SERIES

Car and Driver on BMW Cars 1957-1977
Car and Driver on BMW Cars 1977-1985
Car and Driver on Corvette 1956-1967
Car and Driver on Corvette 1968-1977
Car and Driver on Corvette 1978-1982
Car and Driver on Datsun Z 1600-2000 1966-1984
Car and Driver on Ferrari 1955-1962
Car and Driver on Ferrari 1963-1975
Car and Driver on Ferrari 1976-1983
Car and Driver on Mopar 1956-1967
Car and Driver on Mopar 1968-1975
Car and Driver on Pontiac 1961-1975
Car and Driver on Saab 1956-1985
Car and Driver on Cobra, Shelby &
Ford GT 40 1964-1983

## BROOKLANDS MOTOR & THOROUGHBRED & CLASSIC CAR SERIES

Motor & T & CC on Ferrari 1966-1976
Motor & T & CC on Ferrari 1976-1984
Motor & T & CC on Lotus 1979-1983
Motor & T & CC on Morris Minor 1948-1983

## BROOKLANDS PRACTICAL CLASSICS SERIES

Practical Classics on MGB Restoration
Practical Classics on Midget/Sprite Restoration
Practical Classics on Mini Cooper Restoration
Practical Classics on Morris Minor Restoration

## BROOKLANDS MILITARY VEHICLES SERIES

Allied Military Vehicles Collection No. 1
Allied Military Vehicles Collection No. 2
Dodge Military Vehicles Collection No. 1
Military Jeep 1941-1945
Off Road Jeeps 1944-1971
VW Kubelwagen 1940-1975

## CONTENTS

## ACKNOWLEDGEMENTS

The following is a paragraph from a letter received a few weeks ago from a friend in California:

"Tony Hogg died last Wednesday night (August 3). He went to bed and just never woke up — a heart attack apparently. I had seen him for breakfast Wednesday morning and he seemed fine; looking forward to spending a few days in Wisconsin with his brother-in-law. He was 59, in great spirits and seemingly in good health. I guess we just don't know, do we."

Tony Hogg was an Englishman who emigrated to the US during the 50's. He joined John Bond in the early days of Car Life and Road & Track and rose to become Managing Editor of the latter.

He understood the needs of motorists and especially the hobbyists, who love and cherish their old vehicles and for many years he helped, advised and encouraged us with our reference series. With his great knowledge of the automotive scene he was able to pin-point just what book was needed at a particular time and many of the titles in our current list started from one of his suggestions.

As he was a keen Cobra owner it seemed fitting to compile a book containing a representative selection of his articles and Cobras & Replicas 1962-1983 is dedicated to his memory.

Brooklands Books are produced for owners and restorers, they are printed in small numbers and exist solely because the management of the world's leading journals are cognisant of the needs of these enthusiasts and generously allow us to include their copyright articles.

Cobra devotees will, I am sure, wish to join with us in thanking the publishers of Autosport, Car & Driver, Car Collector, Car Life, Car Preview, Custom Car, Hot Rod, Motor, Motor Sport, Motor Trend, Road & Track, Sporting Cars, Sports Car Graphic, Sports Car World, and Thoroughbred & Classic Cars for their continued support.

R.M. Clarke

ROAD & TRACK
ROAD TEST

# AC-FORD COBRA

*An Ace from AC, assisted by a
V-8 from Ford, is a 150-mph car
built for production racing*

THE DIRECT APPROACH in the production of a high-performance car is to combine a small, light chassis and body, and a big, powerful engine. It may not be subtle, but it is sure-fire, and no one could be better acquainted with this fact than Carroll Shelby. The Pride of Texas has spent a lot of years charging about in all kinds of automobiles and has a fine appreciation of what will, in practical terms, get a person down the road in a hurry. Hence, when Shelby retired from competition driving and began making plans to embark on a venture into automobile manufacturing, it was inevitable that the direct, and effective, approach would be employed.

After due deliberation and prolonged negotiation (the details of which we do not pretend to know) agreements were reached with AC, of England, to make the basic automobile for Shelby, and Ford, of America, to supply engines.

The Cobra's chassis is a very close development of the latest AC "Ace." The frame follows almost exactly the standard AC pattern, having a pair of round-section, tubular main-members running parallel between the box structures,

to which the front and rear suspension links and springs are mounted. However, the tubes in the Cobra frame have a slightly greater wall thickness and there is some extra cross bracing.

All 4 wheels are independently suspended. The suspension consists of A-arms leading from the box structures on the frame to the lower ends of the "uprights" at the wheels and transverse leaf springs (one at each end of the chassis) completing the parallelogram at the upper ends of the uprights.

At Shelby's request, the A-arms and leaf-springs have been lengthened to move the wheels out and widen the tread. The springing has been stiffened by the addition of a "helper" leaf above the main leaf. Also, the rear wheels are given a considerable negative camber to reduce the oversteering effects of the car's rearward weight bias. The suspension system is lacking in some respects, as its parallelogram action tilts the wheels over when the chassis rolls, but it is all-independent, as all too few touring chassis are, and it gives good results.

The AC's usual 16-in. wire wheels are replaced by 15-in. triple-laced, wide-rim wheels. These carry a variety of tires —depending on customer preference—but most of the cars will be Goodyear-shod. Dunlop racing tires will be catalogued as an option but Ol' Shel has said that anything a buyer wants, he will get. We would offer one bit of advice to prospective purchasers; select a tire that gives plenty of tread against the ground; with the Cobra's power/weight ratio, you will need the traction.

Traction will also be needed to get the maximum benefits from the Cobra's braking system. Girling disc brakes are standard, using discs 12 in. in diameter and, although there is no power-booster, the pedal pressure requirements are not too high. On the prototype, the rear brakes were mounted inboard, one on each side of the drive casing, but an outboard mounting will probably be standard on the series-produced cars.

Power for the Cobra is one of Ford's new lightweight V-8s.

It is the largest of the Fairlane-series engines, having a displacement of 260 cu in. and, in single-carburetor form, pushes out an "advertised" 260 bhp. Our test car had the "street" engine, which is virtually stock Ford but equipped with solid valve lifters and a camshaft of non-standard but unspecified timing. We were somewhat surprised to find that it would idle with only a trace of lumpiness, pull strongly at almost any speed, and buzz past the 5800 rpm power peak to 7200 rpm before it began to sound distressed. Also surprisingly, the power did not appear to fall off much even at 7000 rpm—1200 rpm over the point of maximum power.

For the buyer who wants to go racing Shelby has something special under development: a highly tuned competition version of the standard engine with a "top-end-grind" camshaft, higher compression and 4 double-throat Weber carburetors. These are side-draft pattern carburetors, and are mounted on long ram tubes that criss-cross over the top of the engine. In tuned form, the Cobra/Ford engine will produce about 325 bhp, and the added power should do really impressive things for a car that is blindingly fast on 260 bhp.

Special drive components are used all the way through in the Cobra. The transmission is from Borg-Warner (which makes these 4-speed units for Ford) and, although the prototype car had rather wide ratios, Borg-Warner—and Ford—have decided to invest in the tooling for close ratio gearing. Such gearing would eliminate the "gap" that now exists between 3rd and 4th, and the top-end acceleration would be substantially improved. With the present gear staging, the shift into 4th entails a drop in engine speed that would be a serious handicap in competition.

Final drive components—gears, axles, U-joints, etc.—are heavier than those used in the standard AC. A Salisbury drive-gear assembly, of the type used by Jaguar, fits into a housing that is part of the frame (per long-time AC practice) and drives the wheels through Spicer shafts and U-joints. Both shafts and joints have been selected for the strength needed to transmit the power from the Ford engine.

*The Ford Fairlane V-8 fits the AC engine compartment without the proverbial shoehorn.*

Bodywork on the Cobra is almost, but not quite, the same as on the latest AC Ace roadsters. The only change worth mentioning is the flared valance over each wheel well. These are required to provide clearance for the Cobra's large-section tires and widened tread. Shelby is considering making up a few Cobras with AC's Aceca (coupe) body and these would have a top speed even higher than the roadster's.

Within, the Cobra has even more racing-car flavor than is apparent from without. The cockpit (that term exactly describes the passenger area in the Cobra) is quite snug, and the leather-covered bucket seats are real hip-huggers, with lateral support that extends almost from shoulder to knee. Instrumentation is more elaborate than in most racing cars, consisting of speedo, tach, oil-pressure and temperature and water temperature, with a clock, an ammeter and fuel gauge tossed in for good measure (ouch!). The speedo had been removed from the prototype we tested, as the instrument supplie

CONTINUED ON PAGE 19

## ROAD TEST
# AC FORD COBRA

SCALE: 10" DIVISIONS

## DIMENSIONS

| | |
|---|---|
| Wheelbase, in | 90.0 |
| Tread, f and r | 51.5/52.5 |
| Over-all length, in | 151.5 |
| width | 61.0 |
| height | 49.0 |
| equivalent vol, cu ft | 262 |
| Frontal area, sq ft | 16.6 |
| Ground clearance, in | 7.0 |
| Steering ratio, o/a | n.a. |
| turns, lock to lock | 2.0 |
| turning circle, ft | 34 |
| Hip room, front | 2 x 16.5 |
| Hip room, rear | n.a. |
| Pedal to seat back, max | 40.0 |
| Floor to ground | 10.5 |

## CALCULATED DATA

| | |
|---|---|
| Lb/hp (test wt) | 9.6 |
| Cu ft/ ton mile | 175.2 |
| Mph/1000 rpm (4th) | 21.8 |
| Engine revs/mile | 2745 |
| Piston travel, ft/mile | 1315 |
| Rpm @ 2500 ft/min | 5230 |
| equivalent mph | 114.3 |
| R&T wear index | 36.1 |

## SPECIFICATIONS

| | |
|---|---|
| List price | $5995 |
| Curb weight, lb | 2020 |
| Test weight | 2355 |
| distribution, % | 48/52 |
| Tire size | 6.50/6.70-15 |
| Brake swept area (est) | 580 |
| Engine type | V-8, ohv |
| Bore & stroke | 3.80 x 2.87 |
| Displacement, cc | 4261 |
| cu in | 260 |
| Compression ratio | 9.2 |
| Bhp @ rpm | 260 @ 5800 |
| equivalent mph | 127 |
| Torque, lb-ft | 269 @ 4500 |
| equivalent mph | 98 |

## GEAR RATIOS

| | | |
|---|---|---|
| 4th (1.00) | | 3.54 |
| 3rd (1.41) | | 4.99 |
| 2nd (1.78) | | 6.30 |
| 1st (2.36) | | 8.36 |

## SPEEDOMETER ERROR

| | |
|---|---|
| 30 mph | actual, n.a. |
| 60 mph | n.a. |

## PERFORMANCE

| | |
|---|---|
| Top speed (7000), mph | 153 |
| best timed run | n.a. |
| 3rd (7200) | 112 |
| 2nd (7200) | 89 |
| 1st (7200) | 67 |

## FUEL CONSUMPTION

| | |
|---|---|
| Normal range, mpg | n.a. |

## ACCELERATION

| | |
|---|---|
| 0-30 mph, sec | 1.8 |
| 0-40 | 2.5 |
| 0-50 | 3.3 |
| 0-60 | 4.2 |
| 0-70 | 5.4 |
| 0-80 | 6.8 |
| 0-100 | 10.8 |
| Standing ¼ mile | 13.8 |
| speed at end | 112 |

## TAPLEY DATA

| | |
|---|---|
| 4th, lb/ton @ mph | off scale |
| 3rd | off scale |
| 2nd | off scale |
| Total drag at 60 mph, lb | 115 |

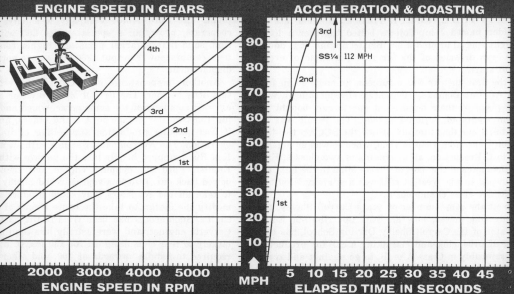

**ENGINE SPEED IN GEARS**

4th
3rd
2nd
1st

ENGINE SPEED IN RPM
2000 3000 4000 5000

**ACCELERATION & COASTING**

3rd
SS¼ 112 MPH
2nd
1st

90 80 70 60 50 40 30 20 10
MPH

ELAPSED TIME IN SECONDS
5 10 15 20 25 30 35 40 45

*DRIVER'S REPORT*  **CARROLL SHELBY'S 260 CUBIC INCH**

W HEN, IN THE EARLY FIFTIES, an English race car builder named John Tojiero bolted together a lightweight special around a hot Bristol engine, it is doubtful if he even dreamed of the far reaching chain of events he was to start.

From the first, the car was a success. So much so, in fact, that the AC Car Company, in search of something new to take the place of their obsolescent sports car, bought the production rights to Tojiero's special. The result was the Ace Bristol, a car that literally owned the SCCA's two-liter Production class from 1955 to 1960, when it was summarily bounced to C-Production, an upgrading of two classes. Even then, in the hands of the likes of Pierre Mion in the East and Pete Haywood in the West, it still was a winner, Mion taking the SCCA class championship.

For about the same number of years Carroll Shelby, former Grade One driver, now an SCG Contributing Editor and operator of the Carroll Shelby Driving School, has been dreaming of producing and marketing a car for production racing, preferably in Class A or B, to go against and try to break the monopoly held in the West by Corvettes and in the East by Ferrari Berlinettas. At the beginning of this year, with announcement of Ford's new 221 and 260 cubic inch lightweight V-8 engines, Carroll knew he had his power

plant. The Ford Motor Company was only too happy to cooperate, providing a special series 260 with a different cam, solid lifters, larger ports and higher compression pistons — horsepower output: 260 bhp or one horse per inch of displacement.

Another happenstance gave Carroll the vehicle to carry this little boomer. The Bristol Motor division of the famous aircraft company of the same name, which had been supplying the two-liter engine to AC and others, announced that it was quitting production and selling of its car building operation. The AC company was left without a power plant. Ken Rudd stepped briefly into the picture with a hopped-up English Ford six cylinder engine and then, apparently, bowed back out. Into this void marched Shelby with an offer to take all the roadsters they could produce if they would modify the design to take the brute torque of the XHP-260 engine. Such swaps had been tried in the past, mostly with Corvette engines, and were usually less than successful due largely to rear ends designed for 130 lbs. ft. of torque being required to handle upwards of 300, and other problems related to doubling and tripling power loadings on something designed to take far less. The AC people were only too willing to oblige. The result was and is the Shelby Cobra, the first of which is seen on these pages. It is the unimproved

*LEFT, lined up, coming out of a tight bend, the Cobra explodes out of the exit but with no snaking or squirrely traits.*

*RIGHT, steer characteristic is neutral if properly driven, but too much gas too soon produces induced understeer.*

*BELOW, lines of the Cobra are similar to Ace-Bristol but nose and tail are longer; 72-spoke, 15-inch wheels used.*

# COBRA

### Class A and B Production, watch out!
PHOTOS: BOB D'OLIVO & DEAN MOON

test prototype but even in its raw form it fulfills Shelby's long standing dream admirably.

Most of the changes in the car, aside from the much stiffer suspension and provision for the V-8 engine with its four-speed Borg Warner gearbox, center around the rear end. This has been beefed up considerably, with heavier hubs and half-axles. The lower A-frames have not only heavier tubing but have been fish-plated as well for extra fore-and-aft stiffness. The long tailshaft of the transmission ends up only inches from the front of the fixed center section, with the result that the drive shaft is little more than a pair of universal joints coupled by a 10-inch length of heavy-wall tubing. The center section itself is a big Salisbury unit similar to that used in the XKE Jaguar. On the prototype this section carries a pair of inboard mounted brakes, with the calipers in trailing position. However, since Shelby does not want to bother with complaints about heat and/or oil leakage on the discs, these will be moved outboard on the production versions.

We spent a day playing with the car and can safely say that it is one of the most impressive production sports cars we've ever driven. Its acceleration, even with the much mal-treated and dynamometer-thrashed single four-throat en-
*(continued)*

*Engine used in prototype car was one of the two Standard units. It differs from the normal 260 Ford in that it has solid lifters, more compression, larger ports and valves.*

*Long tailshaft on gearbox nearly hits rear end; drive shaft is but 10 inches.*

*Gearbox is four-speed Borg Warner; all gears synchronized except reverse.*

*Dash is standard Ace but the tach and speedo are altered for higher speeds.*

*BELOW, setting up for a dynamometer run, crew checks linkage on Webers.*

*ABOVE, bent into a tight corner the Cobra leans slightly but sticks beautifully. BELOW, the optional engine under development on the dynamometer. The four double-choke Webers on ram manifold produced additional 43 bhp by themselves.*

## AC COBRA *(continued)*

gine, can only be described as explosive and at least equal to that of the better running hot Corvettes and Berlinettas we've driven. At one point we entered a clear Freeway in Second gear, giving about three-quarter throttle and by the time we had quartered across to the fast lane the tach was nudging 6000 rpm and we were madly grabbing for Third, looking out for the Law and pulling our right foot off the loud pedal all at the same time.

The rubbery tendency to lean excessively and the slight snaking feel at speed that was exhibited by the Bristol version is gone. While there is some leaning, it is unapparent to the driver and the steer characteristic is dead neutral for the most part, with a mild final oversteer.

Unlike the Ace, however, one cannot punch the throttle in the middle of a turn; wheelspin and a certain amount of false or induced understeer is the immediate effect of too exuberant and too early use of the throttle, particularly in a tight bend. If driven properly through a bend at a steady rate of knots, without excess nudging, the cornering speed is quite high and when the car is lined up for the exit, a poke at the pedal sends the car straight forward with neck-straining velocity. The use of Second gear is necessary only for the tightest turns, Third being sufficient, at least with the 3.54 to 1 rear end, for almost any accelerative need.

As it stands, with the so-called "Standard" engine, similar to the one in the first car, the Cobra will turn up somewhere between 6500 and 7000 in high gear with the 3.54 rear end gearing, which figures out in the near neighborhood of 150 mph. We didn't squeeze it out that hard for several reasons, one being that the tachometer only went to 6000, another being that one doesn't quite dare nudge the Law *that* hard and a third being that it isn't a good idea to thrash a brand new prototype, especially on short acquaintance. Yet, interestingly enough, despite all this potential the car is utterly docile when docility is required, as in city traffic, school zones and the like.

As a car goes, so should it stop. With four-wheel disc brakes with 12-inch discs and 550 square inches of swept area, the Cobra stops very well indeed. On a car that weighs only 1900 pounds soaking wet and ready to go, one might think the car is overbraked. It isn't. The brakes are competition Dunlops, with a rock-hard pedal, and it is almost impossible to lock things up tight. It can be done, but it takes work. A good solid poke at the brake pedal produces a condition just short of lock which hauls the car down far faster and smoother than one would think possible. With its light weight and extreme stopping power, the Cobra should be able to be literally buried into a corner before any drastic stopping action need take place, a great advantage over heavier equipment.

In the production versions an optional engine will be offered for those who wish to do all-out battle against the 327 cubic inch Corvettes and the latest Berlinettas. While the car in Standard configuration will be a Class B contender against the 283's, long-wheelbase Ferrari GTs, Mercedes, Carreras and the like, the optional one can only be classified in Class A wherein the short Ferrari, Corvette 327 and prodified XKE hold sway. Again the 260-inch block is used, spotting all but the Ferrari many cubic inches, especially in the case of the big 'Vette. This one, however, uses an optional cam, 11 to 1 compression, reinforced main bearing caps and is topped off by a quartet of dual-throat side draft 45 DCOE-9 Weber carburetors and a cross-over ram type manifold. Pending final dynamometer tests, we can give only the estimate rendered by Shelby's technical crew: 330 bhp and revs as high as 9000 rpm, although it is doubtful if peak power will be developed anywhere near that high on the scale. More likely peak will be delivered somewhere around 7500, but that can be tailored by changing ram tubes on the carbs and by exhaust pipe lengths, it being planned to offer several optional exhaust systems.

As this is being written, homologation proceedings are being carried out to give the car an FIA classification in the Grand Touring category in standard form and Improved Grand Touring category in optional form. Shelby is making similar arrangements with the SCCA for the same two models to be classified in B and A Production.

First deliveries of the cars will, according to Shelby, start this month, in May, and some orders have already been taken. First come, says Carroll, will be first served. The price? The same as the Bristol version!

For those wishing to cause consternation in the hairy big bore Production ranks, the line forms on the right.

—*John Christy*

## DRIVER'S REPORT

## TEST DATA

| VEHICLE | Shelby AC Cobra | MODEL | 1962 |
| PRICE (as tested) | $5995 FOB, Calif. | OPTIONS | Competition Engine |

### ENGINE:

| | |
|---|---|
| Type | V-8, water-cooled |
| Head | Cast iron |
| Valves | OHV, rocker actuated |
| Max. bhp | 260 @ 6500 rpm |
| Max. Torque | 269 lbs. ft @ 3600 rpm |
| Bore | 3.80 in. |
| Stroke | 2.97 in. |
| Displacement | 260 cu. in., 4262 cc. |
| Compression Ratio | 9.2 to 1 |
| Induction System | Single four throat or quadruple Weber DCOE-9-45 |
| Exhaust System | Headers |
| Electrical System | 12V Lucas |

| CLUTCH: | | DIFFERENTIAL: | |
|---|---|---|---|
| Diameter | 9.5 in. | Ratio | 3.54 to 1. Alt. 2.72 |
| Actuation | Hydraulic | Drive Axles (type) | Open, independent |

| TRANSMISSION: | | STEERING: | |
|---|---|---|---|
| Ratios: 1st | 2.36 to 1 | Turns Lock to Lock | 3 |
| 2nd | 1.78 to 1 | Turn Circle | 31 ft. |
| 3rd | 1.41 to 1 | | |
| 4th | 1.00 to 1 | BRAKES: | |
| | | Drum or Disc Diameter | 12 in. |
| | | Swept Area | 550 sq. in. |

### CHASSIS:

| | |
|---|---|
| Frame | Tube |
| Body | Aluminum |
| Front Suspension | Independent, transverse leaf |
| Rear Suspension | Independent, transverse leaf |
| Tire Size and Type | 6.50-7.00 x 15 Rear; 600 x 15 Front |

### WEIGHTS AND MEASURES:

| | | | |
|---|---|---|---|
| Wheelbase | 90 in. | Overall Length | 165 in. |
| Front Track | 50 in. | Ground Clearance | 5.5 in. |
| Rear Track | 52 in. | Curb Weight | 1890 lbs. |
| Overall Height | 46 in. | Crankcase | 10 qts. |
| Overall Width | 60 in. | Gas Tank | 18 gals., 30 optional |

### PERFORMANCE:

| | |
|---|---|
| Top Speed | (standard) 145 mph; (competition) 175 mph |
| Brake Test | 8.0 Average % G, over 10 stops |
| | No fade encountered |

### REFERENCE FACTORS:

| | |
|---|---|
| BHP per Cubic Inch | 1.0 |
| Lbs. per bhp | 7.2 |
| Sq. In. Swept Brake area per Lb. | 3.45 |

# THE ILLUSTRIOUS AC

### By WAYNE ALLAN

*American racing driver Carroll Shelby is building super-tuned ACs with Ford V8s as the power unit. The car, the Cobra, has a top speed of 150 mph and will accelerate from 0 to 100 mph in 10.8 sec.*

**AC, a small firm manufacturing quality sporting cars, has become a big name in the motoring world because of its link with Carroll Shelby and his Cobra.**

THE fantastic Carroll Shelby/AC Cars Ltd-created Cobra has focused worldwide attention on the highly respected AC.

Many people are asking why they haven't heard much about the firm before this. Yet, this is perhaps only true of enthusiasts outside England, for most sports car minded Britons are well aware of AC's reputation and background.

Actually, AC Cars Ltd has, at times, had the potential to become a much larger firm than it is. Company policy has been resolutely based on producing high quality, medium priced vehicles in conservative quantities.

AC is very much an *owners'* marque, in the tradition of Bentley and Bugatti, and latter-day examples such as Lotus and TVR. The cars, outstanding as they are, owe their commercial existence to knowledgeable and appreciative motorists.

They are by no means run-of-the-mill in either concept or manufacture. Within a modestly styled hand-beaten aluminium body resides a taut frame, an amazing suspension, efficient brakes, a willing engine and rugged transmission.

AC's solid reputation is more than partially built on it being one of the few remaining cars that is equally at home when engaged in everyday motoring or serious competition. Although the firm itself has not actively participated in racing for some time, its laurels are upheld by numerous private owners, particularly in England and the USA.

Throughout the 1920s AC was a force to be reckoned with. During that decade it etched its name in the annals of motor sporting history. An AC was the first 1500 cc car ever to put 100 miles into an hour.

Almost 20 years before AC's race-winning and record-breaking heyday, a car known as the "Weller" was exhibited at the Crystal Palace Show. It created quite a stir, having a 20 hp engine and an aluminium body that was riveted to an aluminium frame — this in the days when most coachwork was wood and fabric.

The project was financed by wealthy butcher John Portwine, and the actual design work was handled by a young and revolutionary engineer,

*The AC Greyhound is a sporting car for the family man. A four seater capable of more than 110 mph, it is built on a lengthened Aceca.*

*Powered by a Zephyr motor the AC 2.6 can be had in five stages of tune. Stage five gives more than 170 bhp, but is only suitable for competition.*

John Weller. Although the car was up to the standards of its competitors, Portwine realised he didn't have sufficient capital to challenge makes such as Mercedes, Napier, Rolls-Royce and Daimler. Instead, he looked for — and found — a promising chink in the market. It was in the requirements of tradesmen and industry that Portwine saw a rewarding field.

At his suggestion, Weller designed a small utility-type vehicle that was destined to oust many horse and cart conveyances. It became the Autocarrier and the firm was renamed Autocar and Accessories Ltd in 1904. The Autocarrier, it has been said, did its job so well that it has never been equalled by any vehicle in its class.

The driver sat just in front of the single rear wheel, above a five horsepower engine, steering the front wheels by tiller. The rear axle, sprung and located by two half elliptic springs, was chain driven directly from the engine. A two-speed epicyclic transmission and multiple-plate clutch were incorporated in the rear hub.

This early forerunner of today's utility-type vehicle soon proved its worth and sales soared.

But the firm's name was too cumbersome. So in 1907 it was abbreviated to AC. By 1910 the AC Sociable had been introduced, derived from the commercial three-wheeler, but with a two-place front seat installed instead of a luggage deck.

The driver was shifted from his rearward perch to sit up front, operating the tiller with his right hand.

Prior to World War One Weller had been busy drawing up an envisaged four-wheeler, to be AC's first of this type, but hostilities forestalled production until 1918. The car had undergone testing at Brooklands in 1913, at that time being powered by a four cylinder side valve Fivet engine from France. Fivet engines were used in the initial production batch of cars in 1918, but supplies were limited as the factory had been bombed by the Germans. With orders streaming in — and too few engines to go round, AC started fitting British Anzanis. Production climbed until AC was taking the entire output of the Anzani factory.

At about this time construction of the rugged little Autocarrier and Sociable ceased, allowing Weller to devote his considerable energy to a project of which traces still exist.

The years immediately preceding 1920 was an era when six cylinder engines became accepted for smooth running and maximum power. Needless to say, Weller had some highly individual ideas of his own on the subject. In 1920 AC produced its six — a beautiful piece of work that was to provide unflagging duty for more than 40 years!

# THE ILLUSTRIOUS AC

### Continued

With a capacity of 2-litres, the AC had a chain-driven single overhead camshaft and wet-type cylinder sleeves. The two rows of inclined valves were operated by rockers, while three siamesed inlet ports entered one side of the cylinder head and six separate exhaust ports left the other. The maximum possible use was made of aluminium alloys, with a result the engine weighed less than 350 lb complete.

Only the manifolds and generator marred what is surely one of the most externally smooth units ever built. Weller not only took pains with the inside, but also insisted that the outside should be free from unsightly lumps, bulges, bolt heads, etc.

The cars to which this engine was originally fitted were not without interest either. They had very short chassis, in relation to their wheelbase, for both axles were located and sprung by half elliptic springs. Torque-tube drive was another feature, as was the three-speed transmission in unit with the live rear axle. Weller also incorporated a disc brake on an extension of the final drive shaft.

The six cylinder AC retained this overall layout until 1933. Between times, however, the firm came under the influence of quick-thinking Australian, S. F. Edge, who took the position of governing director in 1920. Edge was a natural public relations officer, had a flair for publicity and was a real enthusiast. In the early part of his term with AC the famous description "The first light six, and still the finest" came into being.

Under his direction AC built a 1500 cc single overhead camshaft engine (with four valves to each of its four cylinders) specifically to attack the 100 miles in 60 minutes record. Other 1500 cc cars, such as Hillman, Aston Martin, Lagonda and Talbot-Darracq, had come within striking distance of the mark, but it was AC who attained it first. J. A. Joyce drove the record-breaker, putting almost 102 miles into the hour. On some laps he had averaged 104 mph, and he had a maximum speed of 108 mph.

Throughout the following years the marque was deeply entrenched in racing and record-breaking activities. In 1921 AC held over 100 speed and distance records at Brooklands — four times as many as any other car in its class. Then there were 1500 cc records for six, 12 and 24 hours. No less than 77 records and awards were gathered in 1923 and '24. AC's spectacular winning streak continued more or less unabated until Edge retired in 1929 when, without his drive, the company floundered. The depression spurred the decline and the firm went into voluntary liquidation. It was reformed in 1930 by two brothers — W. A. E. and C. F. Hurlock.

Competition activities were, of necessity, curtailed after the revival. The Hurlocks concentrated on restoring the firm to a solid position and in 1933 the 2-litre car underwent extensive modifications. The half elliptic springs were replaced by semi-elliptics, a pressed steel frame was employed, and hydraulic brakes were fitted to the front wheels. The transmission was moved from the rear axle to the engine, resulting in improved roadholding. Three carburettors became standard equipment in 1935 and a four speed gearbox was specified as optional equipment.

In 1936 AC produced a model that has come to be regarded as a classic for the period. It was a short chassis sports two-seater. With normal induction and a 7 to 1 compression ratio, the 2-litre six developed 80 bhp, while another version, fitted with an Arnott supercharger, gave 90 bhp. The unsupercharged model weighed about 21 cwt, had a top speed approaching 90 mph and would accelerate from 0 to 50 mph in 12 seconds.

In 1946 AC was developing a post-war model. Not that much development was required, for most buyers would have been willing to accept the highly regarded pre-war models. That's

*The AC Aceca used the Bristol engine which develops 125 bhp. Although nearly nine years old, it is still modern by present day standards.*

*In the early 1950s, AC brought out a special car for disabled war veterans. The Petite, as it was known, had a top speed of 50 mph and did 70 mpg.*

to each other, slightly over a foot apart, and are joined at various points by crossmembers. The two furthest members are constructed from sheet steel to form box-like structures to which the suspension and final drive housing at the rear is attached.

The suspension follows a familiar pattern at both front and rear. The lower members are tubular A arms, or wishbones, while transverse leaf springs provide the upper location and springing. Telescopic dampers are fitted on all wheels. The final drive and differential assembly is mounted to the frame, the drive being taken to the rear wheels by sliding splined half shafts.

When first introduced the Ace was fitted with the venerable six cylinder AC engine which, at that time, developed 85 bhp. This gave the car a maximum speed of 105 mph, and allowed it to cover the standing quarter mile in 18.0 sec.

Although the Ace was not an inexpensive vehicle, its performance, roadholding, appearance and outstanding quality provided it with a secure place in the sports car world. Catching many enthusiasts on the rebound, AC consolidated its position by announcing the very attractive Aceca coupe version in 1954.

AC was also experiencing success in a far more modest field. During the early post-war years it had secured a contract from the Ministry of Pensions for a light three-wheeler. These were originally intended solely for disabled war veterans, but they proved so practical that they soon found good sales among mini-car buyers. A rear-mounted single cylinder, 350 cc two stroke engine gave a maximum speed of 50 mph and miserly fuel consumption to the order of 60 to 70 mpg.

CONTINUED ON PAGE 55

*The original AC Ace differs only slightly from the latest model. One of the most noticeable changes is the switch from drum to disc brakes on the front All AC's, except Cobra, have drums at the rear.*

virtually what they got anyway. Production centred around two-door four to five seater sedans until more and more clients began asking for versions with open coachwork. These requests were met with a Sports Tourer, followed by a convertible at the 1952 Earls Court Motor Show.

But the 1953 Motor Show was the one that brought enthusiasts to drooling point. AC went modern with 100 mph performance, Italianish styling and the most up-to-date independent suspension all round — the AC Ace was a smash hit!

The frame and suspension, almost identical to that now used in the Shelby/AC-Cobra, was designed by John Tojeiro and developed in Tojeiro sports-racing cars. These potent cars, incidentally, rivalled the superb Lister sports/racing cars of the mid to late 1950s.

The basis is a ladder-type frame fabricated from three inch diameter tubing. Two lengths of this run from front to rear. They lie parallel

# CORVETTE vs. COBRA:
## the battle for supremacy

CONTROVERSY is the lifeblood of automobile racing, and the sport has recently been given another of its frequent transfusions. The big battle now being waged is between factions in the AC Cobra and Corvette Sting Ray camps, with the former's shouts having a decided ring of triumph and the latter's falling about midway between honest outrage and sour grapes. It seems that in a ridiculously short time, the Corvette has been clouted from its position of absolute primacy in large-displacement production-category racing, and Corvette fanciers are a trifle reluctant to accept the new state of affairs. Boosters of the Cobra (few of whom actually have any hope of becoming owners) are the people who have long been annoyed to see those big, ostentatious Corvettes drubbing the *pur sang* imported sports cars. The undeniable fact that the Cobra is as much *bar sinister* as *pur sang* does not appear to bother this group much; the Cobra looks every inch the traditional hand-built sports car (which it is, to a remarkable degree) and that is enough. In any case, the battle waxes furious, and emotional, and it is, therefore, interesting to examine some of the facts in the matter.

When comparing standard street versions of the Corvette and the Cobra, one can see the makings of rather an uneven contest. The Cobra has a curb weight of only 2020 lb, and the latest Ford engine used as standard in the car, the 289-cu-in. Fairlane V-8, has 271 bhp at an easy 6000 rpm. The Corvette presents a slightly confused picture, insofar as the touring version is concerned, because it is offered with engines in several states of tune. However, that most nearly comparable is the one having an engine equipped with the big, 4-throat carburetor, which gives it 300 bhp to propel its 3030 lb. Thus, the "average" Cobra one finds on the street will have a weight to power ratio of 7.45:1, while its Corvette counterpart, even though having more power, is heavier and has a less advantageous ratio of 10.1:1. Moreover, even if the Corvette purchaser is willing to go "whole-hog," and opt for the 360-bhp engine, he will still be hauling about 8.4 lb per bhp. The results are exactly what theoretical considerations predict. The "showroom-stock" Cobra will cut a standing-start ¼-mile in 13.8 sec, with a terminal speed of 113 mph, while a Corvette, in similar tune, is about a full second slower and will reach not quite 100 mph at the ¼-mile mark.

In top speed, too, the Cobra has the advantage. Its nominal frontal area of 16.6 sq ft gives it quite an edge on the Cor-

*SHELBY AC COBRA: all-aluminum, hand-built coachwork on a chassis having a 90-in. wheelbase and powered by a Ford V-8 engine developing up to 340 bhp. It is less than 152-in. long, overall, and weighs only slightly over 2000 lb at curbside, ready to go.*

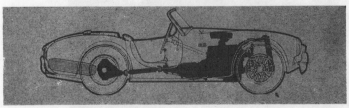

during cornering, and assume a camber angle that adversely affects cornering power. To compensate, the rear wheels, particularly on the competition Cobras, are given a fairly considerable amount of initial negative camber, so that the "outside" wheel is brought upright as the chassis leans, and that restores much of the tire adhesion that would otherwise be lost. Unfortunately, the tires are cambered too much for the best possible grip under straight-line acceleration. And this is no mere theoretical probability; the competition Cobra is notable for the difficulty it has in getting all of its thunderous horsepower applied to the road surface.

The Corvette Sting Ray, on the other hand, is a very recent design, and incorporates much of what has been proven desirable, in general suspension layout, over the past 3 or 4 years. It has the unequal-length A-arm (with coil springs) front suspension that has, with good reason, become standard for both passenger and racing cars, and a Lotus-inspired unequal-length link rear suspension. The roll centers are at a more modern height than is true of the Cobra, 3.25 in. in front and 7.56 in. at the rear. This, in itself, means that the Corvette will tend to lean a bit less than the Cobra, but the really important thing is that the outside wheels are held in a substantially upright attitude as the chassis leans, and the tires maintain good contact with the road. Also, the front suspension has its members angled upward to provide an anti-dive factor of about 50%, which, of course, cuts nose-dip under braking to half of what it would be without this feature. Finally, somewhat softer springs and longer wheel travel are provided in the Sting Ray's suspension, and the car rides more comfortably than the Cobra—which is, itself, not bad in that respect.

We would say that, in the touring versions, the Cobra and Corvette handle about equally well, with a slight nod in the Cobra's direction because of its lower bulk, weight and quicker steering. However, the Cobra's quick steering, now a rack-and-pinion setup in place of the former cam-and-roller steering box, is not entirely a blessing. The completely reversible nature of the steering box delivers road shocks from the tires right through, undiminished, to the steering wheel, and there are times when cornering hard when wheel-fight can be something of a bother. Here again, the Corvette also has its troubles: its steering, although accurate and free of feed-back, is just a shade too slow, and it is sometimes difficult to wind-on opposite lock fast enough to catch the car's tail as it swings out under a too enthusiastic application of power.

With regard to brakes, the Cobra scores heavily over the Corvette—at least insofar as sheer resistance to fade is concerned. Actually, disc brakes have not yet proven to be as trouble-free in day-in, day-out service as the better drum-type brakes, which the Corvette has.

Taken as touring cars, and bearing in mind all of the factors of reliability, service life, availability of service, comfort, utility, and that most important of intangibles, driving pleasure, it is difficult to make a choice. The Cobra is nominally an import, but the major mechanical elements are American manufactured, and most service problems can be handled by

vette, which is pushing away at 19.3 sq ft of air, and the touring version of the Cobra will exceed 150 mph (urk!), about 10 mph faster than the Corvette—even when the Corvette has the "big" engine. This disparity in top speed will continue, in all likelihood. The airflow over the Cobra is probably not as clean as that over the Sting Ray coupe, but the Cobra's advantage in frontal area cannot be denied. To counter that advantage, the Sting Ray would have to be 14% "cleaner" than the Cobra—and it isn't.

In handling, the two cars are more evenly matched than in any other area. Both cars have all-independent suspensions, and any advantage its lightness might give the Cobra in cornering power is just about offset by its rather primitive suspension layout—the Sting Ray has a much more sophisticated suspension.

The Cobra's basic chassis and suspension were laid down back in 1952, or thereabout, by Tojiero, in England, for a series of very limited production sports/racing cars. These were quite successful, and the design was bought by AC and adopted for its 1954 Ace sports/touring car. The Tojiero design, which borrowed heavily from Cooper's serendipitous Formula III car, has a frame that consists of a pair of large (3-in.) diameter steel tubes, with appropriate cross-bracing, and tall box structures at the chassis ends that carry the suspension elements. These elements are a transverse leaf spring, mounted atop the box structures, with a pair of A-arms underneath, giving an essentially parallelogram geometry and a roll center at ground level. This theme is repeated at both front and rear of the chassis.

With this suspension, the Cobra's wheels tilt with the chassis

*CORVETTE STING RAY: futuristic fiberglass panels on a chassis having a 98-in. wheelbase and powered by a Chevrolet V-8 engine developing up to 360 bhp. It is a trifle more than 175-in. long, overall, and weighs slightly over 3000 lb at curbside, ready to go.*

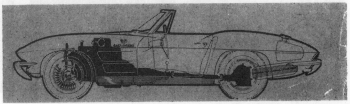

# CORVETTE vs. COBRA:

any Ford garage. It is not outstandingly comfortable, if you happen to be talking in terms of driving from New York to Miami, and not about a sporting afternoon on mountainous back-country roads. Conversely, the Cobra is a somewhat more sporty machine on those same twisty roads than the Corvette. As has been said about so many places, the Cobra cockpit is a great place to visit for fun, but you wouldn't want to live there. As for trunk space, there isn't enough in either of the cars under discussion to argue about.

The Cobra's and Corvette's relative suitability as racing cars is seen in their competition records. Their first meeting, at Riverside Raceway last October, was inconclusive, as the Cobra was then only slightly faster than the "prodified" Corvettes running there, and the Cobra took a narrow lead only briefly, to retire immediately with a broken rear stub-axle. Shortly thereafter, the rivals met again, at Riverside once more, and on that occasion the domination of Corvette in its racing category came to an end. Dave MacDonald and Ken Miles, driving Cobras, beat all of the Corvettes (and there were some good ones there) so badly that it was not even a contest. Indeed, just to add insult to injury, Ken Miles made a pit stop after his first lap, ostensibly to have the brakes, or something, inspected, and after all of the Corvettes had gone by, he set out in pursuit. Whittling away at the Corvettes at the rate of about 5 sec per lap, on a 2.6-mile course, Miles caught his teammate, MacDonald, and relegated the first Corvette to 3rd-place in what seemed like no time at all.

The next confrontation was at the Daytona 3-hour, where a vast comedy of errors prevented the Cobras from defeating the GTO Ferraris (even though they demonstrated that they had the necessary speed) and Dick Thompson, in a Sting Ray, beat back the faltering Cobras to one-up them in that race. In the very recent Sebring Enduro, neither the Cobras nor the Corvettes fared particularly well. A rash of broken engines, and one transmission, eliminated 4 of the 7 Corvettes entered, and one of those still running at the race's end had been in the pits for a majority of the 12 hours having its engine bearings replaced. This Corvette completed only 46 laps.

The showing down at the snake (Cobra) pit was a little, but not much, more impressive; they lost exactly half of the 6 cars entered, and all of the finishing Cobras had to be nursed back from the ranks of the walking wounded at least once during the race. Even so, the Cobras' showing was better than the results indicate. Most of their problems were of a relatively minor nature (no shattered engines or other major components, at any rate), and while they were out on the course the Cobras showed more sheer speed than almost anything there. Phil Hill was observed, in practice, engaging one of the "prototype" Ferraris in a drag race up the pit straight and the good Phil, smiling hugely and rowing away at the gear-lever, carried it to a draw going into the first turn—after

which the Ferrari moved away in no uncertain fashion. The Cobras, while they were in action, had plenty of speed, and the best-placed Corvette finished 10 laps behind the first of the Cobras.

One of the more interesting aspects of the great Cobra-Corvette debate is that the "Chevrolet-Forever" contingent has been complaining bitterly about the "unfair advantage" Shelby has taken in securing a list of approved competition options for his Cobras. This is indeed curious, for the ploy under attack is precisely the one used by GM to make its Corvettes competitive. In fact, we can draw parallels between almost every option offered for both cars. The Corvette has its fuel injection; the Cobra a double brace of 48-mm, double-throat downdraft Weber carburetors. Both have optional competition brakes with friction material largely unsuited to street-type driving. Aluminum alloy, cross-flow radiators are offered for both, as are competition exhaust systems, and cast light-alloy wheels can, due to a relaxing of the production car racing rules this year, be used on any car. Special, and very stiff, springs are catalogued for each car, as are dampers, and there are the miscellaneous items like oversized fuel tanks, for distance events, and more axle ratios than anyone could hope to need for either car. Transmission ratios? They are identical, each car using the same Warner Gear transmission. The Corvette is delivered with the close ratio gears for this gearcase installed as standard, and the wide ratio gears are offered as an option; the Cobra comes standard with wide ratio gears and the close ratio set is available as an option.

In full racing trim, both the Cobra and the Corvette would be thoroughly unpleasant to drive down to the office. The hot-cam, fuel-injected Corvette engine rumbles and chuffs smoke at low speeds, and so does the 340-bhp (at 6500 rpm), Weber-carbureted racing engine in the Cobra. Clutch and brake pedal pressures in both cars are fierce, and the low-end throttle response is awful. The major sin of the Cobra, in the Corvette booster's eyes, is that it is a winner, and it is likely to stay one unless a lightweight version of the Corvette is introduced. These cars' merits as touring machines can be argued, but there is no disputing which is the better racing car. The Cobra's lightness allows it to accelerate and corner faster, and stop quicker (primarily due to the advantage provided by its disc brakes), and on a straightaway of a likely length, the Cobra will be a good 10-mph faster. Given those points, it is very hard to imagine that any well prepared, well driven Cobra will be beaten this year—not by the Corvettes, and possibly not by anyone, unless the organizers get sneaky and push the Cobras over into the same races with all-out racing cars. There are, as a matter of fact, rumors of this happening, and if it does, the Cobras just might beat the big modified cars, too.

No matter where they run, the spectators will be the winners, for the Cobra is fast, noisy and slides about in a spectacular manner, and everyone will eventually learn to admire it for the tremendous sporting/racing machine it is—even the people who drive up to the spectator gate in a Corvette. ⌼

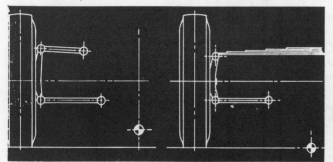

*The Corvette front suspension, left, is more modern and has a higher roll-center than the Cobra's, at right.*

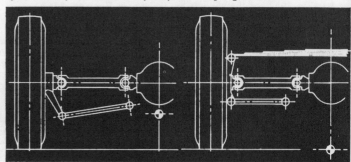

*The Corvette's rear suspension has a higher roll-center than that of the Cobra, which as at the front, uses its spring as a link.*

*A full complement of instruments and a racing steering wheel add a touch of glamour.*

*Bucket seats are a bit too upright, but still are very comfortable.*

*After the spare tire goes in, there isn't too much space left. But it is usable.*

# AC FORD COBRA

**CONTINUED FROM PAGE 6**

by AC had a scale that reached only the 120-mph mark.

Control positioning isn't bad—if you are less than 6 feet tall. The wheel is a bit close for a driver with long arms and the pedals (clutch and brake) are manipulated with one's knees drawn well up. Shelby tells us that he plans adjustments to give more room and we certainly hope this is done. Our tall-ish test driver had his work complicated slightly by the lack of clearance, which resulted in his knees banging against the under edge of the instrument panel with each application of the clutch or brake. Part of this was due to the positioning of the roll-bar in the car; it was placed so that the seat could not be moved back far enough.

In retrospect, we can see that the close-up position of the steering wheel on the prototype may have had its advantages. The Cobra had very quick steering, and what seemed like a lot of caster in the front wheels, and considerable effort is required at the wheel rim to force the car into corners at anything faster than a touring pace. With the wheel in close, it was easier to apply the needed muscle.

*In a demonstration at Riverside Raceway, Carroll Shelby shows photographer Bill Motta 6000 in 4th gear.*

Despite the less-than-perfect control positioning (which should not be true of the series-produced cars) the Cobra's handling was good. With so much power on tap, the inept or inexperienced could get into considerable trouble, but a middlin'-good driver can certainly get the car around a race course in a hurry. One facet of the handling that made us feel a trifle wary at first was the extreme angle (relative to its true line of travel) the car assumes when drifting. There is some oversteer, and when the Cobra is shoved into a turn with brio, the rear wheels creep right out. Treated with any finesse at all, the Cobra will hold its tail-out attitude without trying to spin, but a clumsy throttle foot could give you a thrill.

Insofar as sheer speed is concerned, the Cobra offers more than almost any sports/touring car in the world, and more than any at near its price. Its acceleration, even with the "small" engine, is equal to the best efforts of drag-strip-tuned Corvettes, and it does the job without the benefit of stump-yanker gearing. No special talent is required to get under the 14-sec mark for a standing-start ¼-mile; bang down the throttle-pedal, simultaneously drop in the clutch, and catch the next higher gear each time you reach 7200 rpm. If you persist, the car will accelerate until the tachometer shows 7000 rpm in 4th, which is, without making any allowance for tire expansion, 153 mph. This speed was reached with the car in touring trim, and we were at first reluctant to believe it ourselves. However, we checked and double-checked the accuracy of the tachometer, the gear ratio and the rolling-radius of the tires, and the maximum speed was at least the 153 mph given on the data panel. We cannot give a timed maximum because this test was conducted at Riverside Raceway, which has enough straightaway room to allow the Cobra to reach its top speed, but not enough to permit timing the car over a measured distance at that speed. In fact, some fairly vigorous braking was required to bring the speed down to about 85-90 mph for a drama-free passage through turn 9 at the straightaway's end. As is understandable, we were properly delighted to find that the Cobra's brakes will yank the car down from 150 mph without a trace of wavering or weakness. The brakes are about the best we've ever tried.

Even though something of a hybrid, and lacking in the sort of engine-room niceties that delight the purist, the Cobra is a sports car with more "sport" than almost anything available at any price. Its Ford engine may not have overhead camshafts and lots of polished aluminum castings, but it pumps out the power, it is reliable, and it can be serviced in any little town or hamlet in the country. The styling is "present-day racy," but is clean enough in line to look good for many years. The finish has that hand-wrought appearance that cannot be machine-made and the Cobra looks every bit as good as its price tag. Indeed, we cannot think where more all-around performance can be purchased at the same dollar outlay.

You've heard of the exciting new Cobra? Well, take a gander at Jerry Scheberies'

# MONGOOSE

LEFT – Jerry Scheberies lives here, within plush black leather comfort. The Corvette gearshift lever extends through the tunnel to rear of original lever. Steering wheel is nice looking Derrington model of wood.

Oakland, California

BELOW – In all outward respects, this could be just another AC roadster, except for the brilliant red paint job which could be a giveaway. Borrani wire wheels mount Firestone super sports, front brakes are disc.

*Again, the deceptive lines of the AC breeding serve as a guise to cover what is beneath the sheep's clothing. Those twin tailpipes at the right rear corner might serve to give vent to the secret, but by then Jerry is usually pulling a good lead.*

photos by John O'Donnell

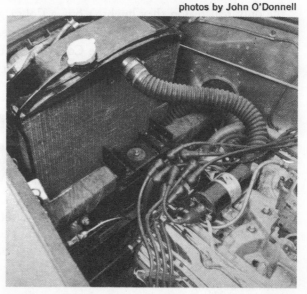

*Like a well fitted glove the F85 Olds engine slips into the '58 AC compartment. The engine swap was accomplished by Jerry and friend Walt Petersen, the only hop up goodies added are Hubbard cam, Forgedtrue pistons, ported heads. The '62 Corvette transmission bolted to F85 engine perfectly.*

*Stock AC front suspension is used with leaf spring riding behind a special radiator fabricated from a 3-inch thick truck core. So far the 1746-pound bomb has turned speeds of 102.8 mph at the strip with e.t.'s in the mid-16's and has won 5 firsts and 25 seconds at Bay Area concours events.*

# ROAD TESTING AN

by Jim Wright, *Technical Editor*

**T**HERE'S NO DOUBT that the AC Cobra is strictly an enthusiast's machine. Since Carroll Shelby first started stuffing the English-built AC chassis full of Ford engine, the car has steadily gained favor with the sports car set and has received some very good reports in the sporty car mags. At this writing, the Cobra is well on its way toward winning the Manufacturers' Trophy awarded by the Sports Car Club of America. Lots could happen between now and the last points race of the year, but at this juncture, the Cobra looks very good.

When we got our test Cobra, we already knew what the enthusiasts thought about it, but we wanted to find out the opinions of non-enthusiast, average drivers. So we chose a dozen people at random (housewives, stenographers, a doctor, a machinist, salesmen, etc.), gave them a go with the car, and recorded their comments.

"It has everything a sports car should have. The power's tremendous, and it has brakes and handling to match. Very impressive. If I could afford a car like this, I'd like it as a second car — just for fun. It *is* a fun car, I think, and certainly not for everyday transportation."

This paragraph is just one of many, but it comes very close to summing up all the comments made by our panel. There were adverse comments, too, the most common being that there's room for only two people. Many would have like roll-up windows and a more substantial top. All of them felt the only real reason they mightn't buy a Cobra would be the high initial cost. All of which adds up to the fact that only the true enthusiasts will be buying this car.

Our personal feelings about the Cobra are that it's indeed a fun car and one that offers unmatched performance in the production car field. Our test roadster, with the exception of a few luxury extras, was the standard offering. Early Cobras were using the 260-cubic-inch Ford Fairlane V-8, but now the standard powerplant is the 289-cubic-inch version. This engine is the same currently offered as a high-performance option for the Fairlane. A solid-lifter cam, four-barrel carburetor, and 11-to-1

## FORD · SHELBY · AC
## COBRA

compression help squeeze out 271 horses at 6000 rpm with 312 pounds-feet of torque at 3400 rpm.

In spite of the tremendous acceleration the package allows, the Cobra is surprisingly docile in city traffic. The camming allows a useful rpm range of 6500, and even though it isn't recommended, you can let rpm fall off to 1000 in high gear, floor the throttle, and find the engine pulling smoothly, without lugging.

During our quarter-mile acceleration runs, we were bothered by excessive wheelspin in first gear and think that with more rubber on the rear, our 0-60 mph times could've been dropped from

# AMERICAN HYBRID

POTENT "289" FORD NESTLES NICELY IN AC CHASSIS, LEAVES ENOUGH ROOM FOR ROUTINE SERVICING. FUTURE MODELS MAY USE ALTERNATOR.

TRACTION WAS BETTER THAN WE'D EXPECTED, ALTHOUGH FULL-THROTTLE FIRST-GEAR STARTS PRODUCED PLENTY OF WHEELSPIN, RUBBER SMOKE.

## FORD-SHELBY-AC-COBRA   *continued*

5.8 seconds down to around five flat. The 0-30 and 0-45-mph marks would also be correspondingly lower. We were very pleased with the quarter-mile averages (104 mph, 13.8-second ET), even though this isn't quite so fast as the near-13-second-flat, 112- to 114-mph figures that have been quoted elsewhere. But our test car wasn't a specially prepared prototype — just a well used demonstrator. Top speed was also shy of the advertised mark of 150 mph. At 5800 rpm in fourth gear (actual 130 mph), the Cobra was just about through. A stretch any longer than the Riverside Raceway backstretch would have allowed more than another three to five miles an hour.

We've driven one of Shelby's full-race Cobras (the "289" engine equipped with four dual-throat, down-draft Italian Weber carbs, plus the usual head and valve modifications allowed in production sports car racing rules), and this one would do an honest 155 mph (7200 rpm with 3.77 gears) at Riverside. That car would also run right at 115 mph in the quarter, with a high 12-second ET. This combination is rated at close to 350 hp but is for racing only and carries a price tag about $2000 higher than the standard model.

Also on tap for the future will be an intake manifold mounting three two-throat carburetors (American manufacture) that will increase horsepower output substantially over that of the standard four-barrel version. The chrome and polished aluminum dress-up kit for the engine is being marketed by Shelby-American Enterprises for all Fairlanes.

The light weight of the AC Ford Cobra combination is the big reason that so much acceleration is possible from a comparatively small 289-inch engine. It's also the weight factor that makes the Cobra a rather economical car to drive. Around town we consistently averaged between 13.5 and 15.1 mpg. Out on the highway, legal limits (65-70 mph) and open, straight, level roads gave a high of 19.3 mpg. It takes a bit of effort to keep the Cobra at legal speeds on the open road because it runs so smoothly and effortlessly in the 80- to 90-mph bracket, and even when driven in this range

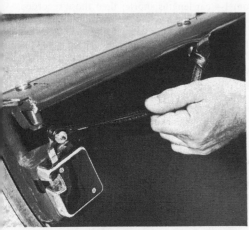

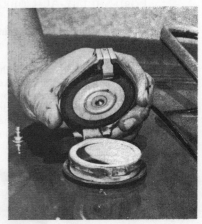

*Door latches are simple but effective. Since Cobra doesn't have roll-up windows, there's no need for outside handles. Doors are light, rigid.*

*Top bow slips easily in place. Top is secured by two windshield latches and a series of snaps at rear. Fitting top is strictly a one-man job.*

*This quick-release gas cap is standard equipment. Straight-in fill neck gives fast gassing.*

*(ABOVE) Sliding plexiglass windows are standard, help make Cobra an all-weather car. Plastic wind wings divert air, are very worthwhile options.*

PHOTOS BY BOB D'OLIVO

*(RIGHT) Cockpit is well fitted and features full instrumentation, top-grade leather buckets, and adjustable wood-rimmed aluminum steering wheel.*

**HANDLING CHARACTERISTICS OF THE COBRA ARE A MATCH FOR CAR'S ACCELERATION, AND TOP-SPEED POTENTIAL WILL SUIT MOST DRIVERS.**

## FORD-SHELBY-AC-COBRA  *continued*

for any distance, fuel consumption didn't fall below 16.1 mpg. Overall average for over 1500 miles of all kinds of driving was 14.1 mpg.

When we were recording the comments of our panel, the Cobra's four-wheel disc brakes seemed to arouse as much admiration as did the car's power. This surprised us, because we didn't think the average driver was aware that the drum brakes on his (or her) domestic car weren't all that they could be. The Cobra's stopping distances from 60 mph are as quick as any we've recorded with any other disc-braked

*Tool kit includes brass knock-off hammer for the wire wheels. Luggage compartment offers a surprising amount of usable space.*

*Twelve-inch discs, used front and rear, give the Cobra plenty of stopping power. Rear unit (left) includes the parking brake.*

car and are from 1-4 car lengths shorter than those recorded with drum-braked cars. Our stops were absolutely straight-line, which in these days of tightly packed four-lane freeways is a big plus factor. At the end of our high-speed runs (as well as at the end of the quarter-mile acceleration runs) we used the brakes with maximum effort and survived every stop without any apparent fade. Pedal pressure increased as the heat went up, but the brakes could be locked at will any time during our stops. The parking brake doesn't have the *really on* feel that a drum parking brake has, and the lever has to be pulled right to the last notch before it'll hold. But it will hold.

Although a 49/51 weight distribution suggests a bit of oversteer, the chassis actually has quite a bit of understeer built into it. At low speeds in tight corners, it's as excessive as any domestic sedan, but as the cornering speed goes up, the degree of understeer diminishes to the point where handling is fairly neutral. Oversteer can be induced at almost any point in a corner with the throttle, but if you reach the point where the chassis moves naturally from neutral steel to oversteer, you've lost it. While most of our panel thought the Cobra was very comfortable at speed, they also thought it rode like a truck at slower speeds. We agree, but personally we wouldn't sacrifice any of the Cobra's high-speed sureness and safety for low-speed comfort.

We'd like to say that this car is one in which you could blast through a 600-mile day with no ill effects, but we can't. We found the combination of severe wind buffeting (without the top or without the side curtains) excessive. Engine heat in the cockpit (even on mild days) plus high wind, road, and engine noise level, and a driver's seat that's not nearly as comfortable as it should be became fatiguing after as little as 150 to 200 miles. There's a limit to our enthusiasm.

The top, at best, is strictly an emergency measure. It balloons badly at almost all speeds, causing great gaps to open up around the tops of windows. It also slaps and booms at a terrific rate. On the other hand, it's a very simple matter for one man to put up or take down. When not in use, it's stowed in the trunk which, by the way, is large enough to accommodate the luggage needs of two people, with room to spare. The side windows are plastic, and the rear half slides forward for ventilation.

The English leather-covered bucket seats are deep and hip hugging, but they lack comfort because the seat back is too straight. With two or three degrees of backward rake, it'd be perfect. There isn't a lot of leg room, but we found it adequate for our five-eleven-and-a-half frame. Fore-and-aft seat adjustment plus an additional three inches' adjustment on the wood-rimmed steering wheel will allow most

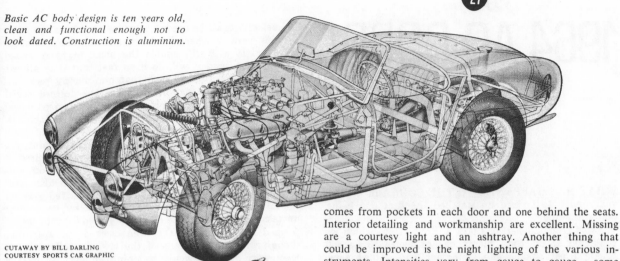

*Basic AC body design is ten years old, clean and functional enough not to look dated. Construction is aluminum.*

CUTAWAY BY BILL DARLING
COURTESY SPORTS CAR GRAPHIC

drivers to find a position to their liking. Rearward visibility isn't the best with the top up. External accessory mirrors would solve this problem.

Instrumentation is complete. The large tachometer and speedometer are easy to read at speed, and other instruments are oil pressure, oil temp, water temp, ammeter, fuel level, and clock. The map case in the dash is large and has a locking door. Further interior storage space

comes from pockets in each door and one behind the seats. Interior detailing and workmanship are excellent. Missing are a courtesy light and an ashtray. Another thing that could be improved is the night lighting of the various instruments. Intensities vary from gauge to gauge — some barely discernible and others extremely bright.

The handformed aluminum body reflects quality workmanship from front to rear, and the paint is smooth and even. The hood latches on the test car were extras and eliminated the use of a key to open the hood.

With a p.o.e. price of $5995, the Cobra doesn't come cheap, but if you fancy yourself an enthusiast and you want to get the most out of your dollar, we'd recommend a serious look and a personal test drive in this car.    /MT

## AC COBRA
### 2-door, 2-passenger roadster

**OPTIONS ON CAR TESTED:** Chrome wire wheels, wind wings, luggage rack, engine dress-up kit, hood latches, tuned chrome air cleaner, heater, front and rear guards, sun visors, seat belts

**BASIC PRICE:** $5995 p.o.e.
**PRICE AS TESTED:** $6610 (plus tax and license)
**RECOMMENDED ENGINE RED LINE:** 7200 rpm

### PERFORMANCE

**ACCELERATION** (2 aboard)
0-30 mph ...............................2.7 secs.
0-45 mph ...............................4.0
0-60 mph ...............................5.8

Standing start 1/4-mile 13.8 secs. and 104 mph
Speeds in gears @ 7200 rpm
1st ................68 mph    3rd ................113 mph
2nd ................90 mph    4th ................130 mph
(actual top speed @ 5800 rpm)

Speedometer Error on Test Car
Car's speedometer reading ......28  44  49  60  71  81
Weston electric speedometer ....30  45  50  60  70  80

Observed miles per hour per 1000 rpm in top gear .............22.2 mph
Stopping Distances — from 30 mph, 35 ft.; from 60 mph, 128 ft.

## SPECIFICATIONS FROM MANUFACTURER

**Engine**
Ohv V-8
Bore: 4.0 ins.
Stroke: 2.87 ins.
Displacement: 289 cu. ins.
Compression ratio: 11.0:1
Horsepower: 271 @ 6000 rpm
Torque: 312 lbs.-ft. @ 3400 rpm
Horsepower per cubic inch: 0.93
Ignition: 12-volt coil

**Gearbox**
4-speed manual, all-synchro; floor-mounted lever

**Driveshaft**
One-piece, open tube

**Differential**
Hypoid
Standard ratio: 3.54:1

**Suspension**
Front: Independent, with lower wishbones, single transverse leaf springs, direct-acting tubular shocks, and anti-roll bar
Rear: Independent, with lower wishbones, single transverse leaf spring, direct-acting tubular shocks

**Steering**
Worm and sector
Turning diameter: 34 ft.
Turns: 1¾ lock to lock

**Wheels and Tires**
Center-lock wire wheels
6.00/6.40 x 14 4-ply nylon
Goodyear Bluestreak tires

**Brakes**
Girling hydraulic discs
Front: 12-in. cast-iron discs
Rear: 12-in. cast-iron discs (parking brake incorporated in calipers)
Total swept area: 580 sq. ins.

**Body and Frame**
Tubular ladder-type frame with separate handformed aluminum body
Wheelbase: 90.0 ins.
Track: front, 51.5 ins.; rear, 52.5 ins.
Overall length: 151.5 ins.
Curb weight: 2350 lbs.

# 1964 AC COBRA

**ROAD TEST 26/63**

**SPORTS CAR** GRAPHIC

*Shelby Improves the Breed Of His Firmly-Established War Horses*

WHAT HAS HAPPENED TO THE COBRA in the last year and a half since we watched the first one being bolted together?

Aside from clobbering Class A Production, which we predicted at the time, plenty has happened to Carroll Shelby's pet snake. The youngster has gained some weight (but in the right places), gotten some new gear ratios, gained 29 more cubic inches in the powerhouse and, most recently, a new steering system with a fancy new wheel to go with it. All of these refinements add up to a civilizing influence without taming the beast more than a little bit.

Top speed is down from the original 154 mph in the street machine for the very simple reason that such top end velocity can't be used. It's still available in the competition version where it can be and obviously is used, however. It will still double the usual highway speed limit though, and it will do it so fast that it is almost unbelievable. Torque is such that one merely picks an intermediate gear, instantly reaches the desired speed and then drops it into high gear, be that desired speed 20 mph or 120 mph. It is also totally controllable, so much so as to be unbelievable to the watcher of such doings. One incident should suffice to make the point. We were stopped at a light one evening during the course of the test. The light changed to green and we were off, getting instantly to the 40 mph limit in that particular area. A minute or so later there was an ominous red glow in the mirror. Quite obviously we had attracted some very unwelcome attention. We dutifully pulled over to be informed that we had NOT been clocked for speeding, though when the minions of the law took off after us they were sure we would be doing at least 80 by the time they could settle down for clocking. They were just curious, it seemed, so we did what we could to satisfy their curiosity. What really bothered them, since they had seen quick machines before, was the total absence of tire squeal during that take-off.

We ourselves hadn't really noticed this factor but it is true. Unless you try very hard the Cobra does not light the tires up, squeal or do much of anything in this

nature; it just turns everything into forward motion right now. Except where there is a puddle of water involved. If more than the tiniest bit of exuberance is used around water it gets a bit like feeding an oily snake to a greased pig. It's all right if you know what you're doing and are prepared for it but if done inadvertently the word "busy" acquires a new and very significant meaning.

All of this, of course, isn't really anything new; virtually every Cobra from Ol' Number One to the latest one are like that. The newer ones are just a little more so.

What *is* striking is the new steering. With the earlier worm-and-peg type of steering the control was progressive. The further the steering wheel was turned the faster the angularity change became on the front wheels. A fairly large movement in the dead ahead position produced a fairly small change in direction, quick but not twitchy. A little more turn created a proportionately larger change in direction and more turn still produced an even greater change. It wasn't annoying but it was there; it was something to get used to and also took a certain amount of muscle on a tight slow turn. Now the car has been fitted with rack and pinion steering. It doesn't turn any quicker, or any slower either, but it's a great deal easier and because it lacks the progressive feature of the earlier system, a given turn of the wheel produces the same effect at

any point. It makes the car feel much lighter although it is actually close to 200 pounds heavier than the prototype.

Ride at low speeds, especially over choppy pavement, is on the harsh side but as the speeds go up things begin to smooth out and one is quite willing to put up with the slight harshness for the stability at higher velocities. Perhaps because of this greater comfort at speed, and also because of that acceleration, attention must be paid to the instrument panel if contretemps with the law are to be avoided.

Handling characteristics in the '64 version are little changed over that of the earlier versions. The car is basically a mild understeering vehicle that graduates to neutral steer as speeds go up. This neutral steering can be changed at will at almost any speed to an induced oversteer by judicious use of the throttle, but if allowed to progress through the neutral stage to a final oversteer, you've lost it. The car is also quite tire-sensitive, responding definitely to changes in tire tread design and compound hardness both in the street version and in competition form. Original equipment for the street machine is, currently, the Goodyear Wingfoot. Our test car was, at first, equipped with the prototype of a tire, also by Goodyear, that is similar in design though with a more complicated tread pattern that gave more lateral stability, especially in the wet. Quite possibly later

# AC COBRA

A bit heavier, but sporting more inches and new steering, is the latest Cobra version.

The potent and compact Fairlane is now 29 inches larger (289 cu. in.) and has special short-branch exhaust manifolds that make it an 8-into-4-into-2 setup.

Top, a handsome wood-rimmed steering wheel is new addition. Directly above, luggage space is more than adequate in neatly-finished rear compartment.

The new rack-&-pinion steering gear—nestled between front spring and radiator—corrects the Cobra's geometry and makes steering through corners like above quite effortless. Strong horsepower/weight ratio makes throttle-steering easy, also.

Cobras will be equipped with these as they become available. Another tire that would seem to make sense might well be the Pirelli Cinturato; another might be the Dunlop SP if it becomes available in this country.

In terms of personal comfort the Cobra is more than adequate. Seats, though rather upright are well padded and offer extremely good support. The cockpit is fully upholstered and extremely well equipped in terms of instruments and stowage space. Legroom is more than adequate, particularly regarding length, though the large center tunnel does restrict sideways movement. There is a large, lockable dash compartment for hard-goods and valuables; other gear can be stowed under the dash on the tunnel and to some extent behind the seats. Virtually everything in the way of small and large controls is easily reached by the driver. One change in the new versions is that the adjustable steering column has been discontinued. However, with the lightened steering it really doesn't make much difference since an arms-out position is quite comfortable. The earlier version wanted some shoulder pressure which made the adjustable feature a necessity. With the rack and pinion set-up it becomes unnecessary.

Another improvement, minor but noticeable, that has been made in the 18 months the car has been around, is in the pedals. One would expect that a large, hairy car would have large, hairy pedal pressures and such was the case with the prototype. Not so with these later versions, even with the '63 cars, one of which we drove for comparison. While not exactly power-assisted light, they don't leave one with charliehorses in the calf and thigh muscles either. They're firm but not stiff and the degree of control is excellent. As with any full disc brake layout some pressure is needed, but any and all stops are made easily and without panic, wheelfight or even wheel lock. In fact trying to lock the wheels solidly under braking is as hard as trying to spin them on take-off. It can be done but it takes doing. In short the car just stops, right now, without any fuss or bother.

Some reviewers have made remarks about the minimal weather protection. How times have changed! First and foremost, the Cobra is a sports car of the traditional variety, perhaps the last of the breed of big, hairy, fast wind-in-the-face roadsters. The weather equipment is there for use in inclement weather which means it will keep off the rain, hail or what-have-you. In short the Cobra is a sports car, one of the best in the world, and it doesn't pretend to be anything else. —*John Christy*

PHOTOS: BOB D'OLIVO

Rear view; what competitors saw most of in the U.S. Manufacturer's Championship events. Cobra won hands-down.

---

**ROAD TEST 26/63**

**SPORTS CAR GRAPHIC**

## AC COBRA 1964

PRICE (as tested) .................... $5995.00 L.A.

### ENGINE:

| | |
|---|---|
| Type | Ford Fairlane V-8 high/performance |
| Head | Cast iron, removable |
| Valves | OHV, pushrod/rocker |
| Max. bhp | 271 @ 5800 rpm |
| Max. Torque | NA |
| Bore | 4.0 in. 101.5 mm. |
| Stroke | 2.87 in. 73 mm. |
| Displacement | 289 cu. in. 4734 cc. |
| Compression Ratio | 11.0 to 1. |
| Induction System | Single 4-bbl |
| Exhaust System | Headers (8-into-2) |
| Electrical System | 12V distributor |

**CLUTCH:**
Heavy-duty single disc, dry
Diameter ............ N.A.
Actuation ............ Hydraulic

**DIFFERENTIAL:**
Spring
Ratio .................... 3.78 to 1
Drive Axles (type) ... Open, 2-joint, slip-coupled

**TRANSMISSION:**
Full-synchro 4-speed light-alloy ease
Ratios: 1st ............ 2.20 to 1
2nd ............ 1.64 to 1
3rd ............ 1.31 to 1
4th ............ 1.0 to 1

**STEERING:**
Rack & pinion
Turns Lock to Lock ......... 2⅞
Turn Circle ................. N.A.

**BRAKES:**
Girling disc
Disc Diameter ............ 11 in.
Swept Area ......... 580 sq. in.

### CHASSIS:

| | |
|---|---|
| Frame | Single tube steel |
| Body | Aluminum |
| Front Suspension | Single lower "A," transverse leaf upper, tube shocks |
| Rear Suspension | Single lower, transverse leaf upper. tube shocks |
| Tire Size & Type | 7.35 x 15 Goodyear G8'5 |

### WEIGHTS AND MEASURES:

| | | | |
|---|---|---|---|
| Wheelbase: | 90 in. | Ground Clearance | 5.5 in. |
| Front Track | 51.5 in. | Curb Weight | 2030 lbs. |
| Rear Track | 52.5 in. | Test Weight | 2310 lbs. |
| Overall Height | 49.0 in. | Crankcase | 9 qts. |
| Overall Width | 61.0 in. | Cooling System | N.A. |
| Overall Length | 151.5 in. | Gas Tank | 17 gals. |

### PERFORMANCE:

| | | | |
|---|---|---|---|
| 0-30 | 2.5 sec. | 0-70 | 8.0 sec. |
| 0-40 | 3.7 sec. | 0-80 | 11.5 sec. |
| 0-50 | 4.9 sec. | 0-90 | 13.5 sec. |
| 0-60 | 6.7 sec. | 0-100 | 17.9 sec. |

Standing ¼ mile .................... 14.9 sec. @ 93 mph
Top Speed (av. two-way run) .................... 148 mph

| Speed Error | 30 | 40 | 50 | 60 | 70 | 80 | 90 |
|---|---|---|---|---|---|---|---|
| Actual | 30 | 40 | 50 | 59 | 69 | 79 | 89 |

Fuel Consumption: Test ........ 12 mpg     Average ........ 17 mpg

Recommended Shift Points
Max. 1st .................... 52 mph     Max. 3rd ................. 87 mph
Max. 2nd .................... 70 mph
RPM Red-line .................... 5500 rpm

Speed Ranges in gears:
1st .................... 0 to 52 mph     3rd .................. 12 to 87 mph
2nd .................... 5 to 70 mph     4th .................. 15 to top mph
Brake Test .................... 72 Average % G, over 10 stops
No Fade encountered

### REFERENCE FACTORS:

| | |
|---|---|
| BHP per Cubic Inch | 0.937 |
| Lbs. per bhp | 7.5 |
| Piston Speed @ Peak rpm | 2770 |
| Sq. In. Swept Brake area per Lb. | 0.285 |

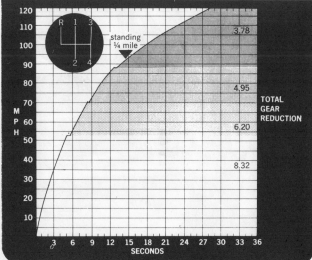

standing ¼ mile

TOTAL GEAR REDUCTION
3.78
4.95
6.20
8.32

SECONDS

# COBRAS AREN'T LUCKY...

...They're just the best. Alfred Neubauer, the famous racing manager for the all conquering Mercedes-Benz team of a few years back, was once quoted as saying "successful racing is the elimination of luck." This "elimination of luck" in a championship production sports/racing car is by no means a simple task. A good portion of it, however, can be attributed to the 289 cubic inch "high performance" Ford Fairlane V-8 which powers the COBRA. Although delivering close to 380 h.p. in racing tune the COBRA engine has been one of the most reliable factors contributing toward the COBRA'S fantastic racing success.

COBRAS won all *three* Road Racing Championships open to their class in 1963! The privately entered COBRAS of Johnson and Brown won first and second in the coveted Sports Car Club of America *"A" Production Championship.* Bob Holbert and Ken Miles placed first and second in the U.S. Road Rac-

ing *Drivers Championship* while the COBRA factory racing team won the *United States Road Racing Championship* with a total of 111 points*. What makes this unprecedented display of victory even more impressive is that 1963 was the COBRA'S first year of production! In this one short year the COBRA has proven itself the "Car to Beat" and has become the unparalleled standard by which other production sports cars are judged.

It takes great courage for a relatively small manufacturer (two cars per day) like Shelby American to enter open competition against the best the world has to offer. For on the success or failure of such a venture rides the future of the company. This spirit, however, reflects the dynamic vitality and sound racing experience of that closely knit group of men responsible for the COBRA, for they are the "Eliminators" of that intangible called luck.

*Ferrari 28 pts.   Chevrolet 19 pts.   Jaguar 12 pts.

## COBRA
### POWERED BY FORD

SHELBY AMERICAN, INC. 1042 PRINCETON DRIVE, VENICE, CALIFORNIA

# AC COBRA

*The street version of this famous machine is also long on performance*

WHEN CARROLL SHELBY retired from racing in 1960, he turned his considerable energy and experience to the production of a sports car incorporating his own ideas, and the result was the AC Cobra. In order to prove the car, he immediately engaged in an extensive racing program, which has put his brainchild in the winner's circle at numerous circuits, and enabled him to sell all the street models that the AC company is able to produce.

The idea of combining a big American V-8 with an English sports car chassis is certainly not new. Sidney Allard had a good run for his money in the early Fifties and, although it might appear that Shelby has taken over where Allard left off, the Cobra is in fact a much more sophisticated automobile, and its racing successes are being achieved at a time when the competition is a lot tougher than was the case

## AC COBRA
### *AT A GLANCE...*

| | |
|---|---|
| Price as tested | $6343 |
| Engine | V-8, 4738 cc, 271 bhp |
| Curb weight, lb | 2170 |
| Top speed, mph | 139 |
| Acceleration, 0-60 mph, sec | 6.6 |
| Passing test, 50-70 mph, sec | 2.5 |
| Overall fuel consumption, mpg | 15 |

# AC COBRA

when the Cadillac and Chrysler Allards were in their prime.

Although the prototype AC Cobra was little more than a standard AC chassis and body with a Ford engine and transmission dropped into it, much development work has been done since, and many of the lessons learned while Shelby's team have been racing the cars have been incorporated in the design. One does not really appreciate what Shelby has done to the AC design until one sees an AC Bristol and compares it to a Cobra. The AC Bristol is a nice, lean, graceful car, and the Cobra is a squat, mean and brutal piece of machinery, but nevertheless extremely handsome.

The basis of the Cobra is the AC chassis designed by John Tojeiro in 1954. The frame itself is extremely simple, consisting of two large-diameter tubes with sturdy cross members front and rear and an additional member at the transmission. The aluminum body is supported by a framework of small-diameter steel tubes, and the body is not stressed at any point. The suspension is fully independent with transverse leaf springs front and rear and lower A-arms. The result is a rugged but simple structure which is well able to withstand the torque of the 4738-cc Ford engine. However, both the chassis and the suspension have been modified and these modifications are mainly concerned with strengthening various components. The wall thickness of the frame tubing has been increased slightly, the A-arms strengthened, an additional spring leaf incorporated front and rear, and Texas-size universal joints installed, among other modifications.

The engine used in the street model Cobras is the 271-bhp version of the 289-cu-in. Ford engine which is offered as an option on certain Ford sedan models. This engine features a high lift cam, bigger valves, a single 4-barrel carburetor, mechanical valve lifters, and a compression ratio of 11.6:1. In this form it presents an excellent compromise for street use because its power output is about as much as one can use in the Cobra, but it is still both docile and reliable. For those people who want even better performance, a variety of Cobra options are offered for the engine, and the ultimate modification is a set of four Webers with manifolding which sell for an additional $1230.70, although they are not recommended for street use.

Coupled to the engine is a Warner Gear T-10 transmission which is undoubtedly one of the best all-synchro 4-speed transmissions we have ever sampled, and is quite strong enough to handle the power of the engine under the most arduous sports car driving conditions. The combination of engine and gearbox makes a lot of sense because parts and service are readily available throughout the country, and both components do their job exceptionally well.

At first sight, the Cobra gives the impression of being definitely a man's car, and this is borne out by its performance

*271-bhp Ford engine provides startling performance.*

*Trunk space is sufficient for one large suitcase.*

## ROAD TEST
# AC COBRA

SCALE: 10" DIVISIONS

### PRICE

List, West Coast POE.......$5995
As tested, West Coast......$6343

### ENGINE

Engine, no. cyl, type.....V-8, ohv
Bore x stroke, in......4.00 x 2.87
Displacement, cc...........4730
   Equivalent cu in.........288.5
Compression ratio.........11.6:1
Bhp @ rpm.........271 @ 6000
   Equivalent mph............121
Torque @ rpm, lb-ft..314 @ 3400
   Equivalent mph.............69
Carburetor, no., make.1-4-bbl Ford
Type fuel required.....Premium

### DRIVE TRAIN

Clutch diameter & type:....10.41
   Semi-centrifugal
Gear ratios, 4th (1.00)......3.77
   3rd (1.41)................5.32
   2nd (1.78)................6.71
   1st (2.36)................8.90
Synchromesh............on all 4
Differential ratio..........3.77

### CHASSIS & SUSPENSION

Frame type: large diameter, ladder-type tube frame.
Brake type................disc
   Swept area, sq in......est. 580
Tire size.............7.35 x 15
   Wheel revs/mi............788
Steering type......rack & pinion
   Turns, lock to lock.........2.0
   Turning circle, ft..........34
Front suspension: Independent with A-arm, transverse leaf spring, tube shocks.
Rear suspension: Independent with A-arm, transverse leaf spring, tube shocks.

### ACCOMMODATION

Normal capacity, persons.........2
Hip room, in.........2 x 16.5
Head room................35.5
Seat back adjustment, deg.....0
Entrance height, in..........41
Step-over height.............14
Floor height..............10.5
Door width...............29.5
Driver comfort rating:
   for driver 69-in. tall.......65
   for driver 72-in. tall.......55
   for driver 75-in. tall.......50

### GENERAL

Curb weight, lb........ . . 2170
Test weight................2540
Weight distribution
   with driver, percent .... 47/53
Wheelbase, in............90.0
Track, front/rear.....51.5/52.5
Overall length............151.5
   Width....................61.0
   Height...................49.0
Frontal area, sq ft.........16.6
Ground clearance, in.........5.0
Overhang, front..........30
   Rear...................39
Departure angle, no load, deg .18
Usable trunk space, cu ft......5.5
Fuel tank capacity, gal........18

### INSTRUMENTATION

Instruments: 160-mph speedometer, 8000-rpm tachometer, oil temp, water temp, oil pressure, fuel, clock, ammeter.
Warning lamps: turn indicators, generator, high beam.

### MISCELLANEOUS

Body styles available: roadster as tested.

### ACCESSORIES

Included in list price: 271-bhp engine, 4-speed gearbox, full instrumentation, • wire wheels, limited-slip differential.
Available at extra cost: grille guard, wind wings, visors, heater, seat belts, luggage rack, chrome wheels, outside mirror, radio—plus many performance options.

### CALCULATED DATA

Lb/hp (test wt)..............9.4
Cu ft/ton mi.............196.9
Mph/1000 rpm (4th).......20.2
Engine revs/mi............2970
Piston travel, ft/mi........1421
Rpm @ 2500 ft/min........5230
   Equivalent mph..........103
R & T wear index..........42.2

### MAINTENANCE

Crankcase capacity, qt.........5
   Change interval, mi.......5000
Oil filter type............paper
   Change interval, mi.......5000
Lubrication grease points.......8
Lube interval, mi..........1000
Tire pressures, front/rear, psi ..28

# ROAD TEST RESULTS

### ACCELERATION

0–30 mph, sec................2.2
0–40 mph...................3.4
0–50 mph...................5.0
0–60 mph...................6.6
0–70 mph...................8.6
0–80 mph..................10.8
0–100 mph.................14.1
Passing test, 50–70 mph......2.5
Standing 1/4 mi, sec........14.0
   Speed at end, mph.......99.5

### TOP SPEEDS

High gear (6900), mph.......139
3rd (7000)................100
2nd (7000)................79
1st (7000)................60

### GRADE CLIMBING

(Tapley Data)

4th gear, max gradient, %.....28
3rd.................off scale
2nd.................off scale
Total drag at 60 mph, lb......115

### SPEEDOMETER ERROR

30 mph indicated.... actual 31.0
40 mph...............41.3
60 mph...............62.6
80 mph...............83.0
100 mph..............104.4

### FUEL CONSUMPTION

Normal range, mpg.........13–18
Cruising range, mi......230–320

## ACCELERATION & COASTING

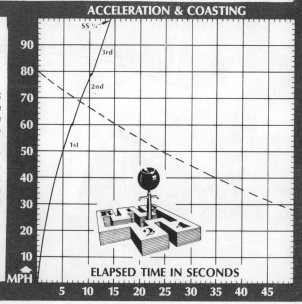

SS 1/4

3rd

2nd

1st

ELAPSED TIME IN SECONDS

MPH

90 80 70 60 50 40 30 20 10

5 10 15 20 25 30 35 40 45

and handling characteristics. However, the standard of finish of both the exterior and interior are very good and the aluminum body shows evidence of a considerable amount of hand workmanship. Unfortunately, the car does not offer very much in the way of creature comforts for its $6000. There are no windup windows and the top is a tent-like affair which one assembles around a collapsible frame carried in the trunk. The result is minimal weather equipment reminiscent of the MG-TC. On the other hand, the interior is carpeted and the bucket seats are covered with leather, although they are not particularly comfortable because the back seems to be far too upright. Furthermore, the taller driver will find that there is hardly sufficient room to operate clutch, brake and throttle.

On the road the Cobra is a curious mixture of ancient and modern. It is without doubt one of the fastest cars we have ever tested, and one can forgive almost anything for the sheer exhilaration of its performance. On the other hand, the suspension and steering reminded us of the sports cars we were driving 10 years ago, which is not necessarily a criticism. In an age when the sports car is expected to offer all the comforts of a family sedan, it is pleasant to revert to something like the Cobra which is nothing more than a weapon designed specifically for proceeding from one point to another in the minimum amount of time.

At low speeds both the suspension and steering are stiff, and it is not possible to tell that the rear suspension is independent. However, when the car is being driven in the manner for which it is designed, the road holding, steering and directional stability are very good. The behavior of the suspension is distinctly peculiar when the car is driven hard because the parallelogram layout at front and rear causes the wheels to lean excessively when cornering. This is particularly noticeable if one watches one of the competition cars during a race, however, the effect on the road holding is not as bad as it appears at first sight.

To compensate in part for the peculiarities of the suspension, the street Cobras are equipped with 7.35 x 15 Goodyear tires (Shelby handles Goodyear racing tires as a sideline), and apart from improving the road holding by the simple method of putting more rubber on the ground, they are a great asset to a car which needs all the traction it can get. This is carried a stage further in the competition models which are equipped with monstrous 8.20 x 15 Goodyear Stock Car Specials. Another noticeable feature of the street machines when viewed from the rear is the 3 degrees negative camber designed to counteract a tendency toward oversteering.

Although oversize tires are a definite improvement, they do tend to make the steering heavy at low speeds, but another side effect is that they contribute directly to the cars remarkable stopping ability which is insured by the Girling disc brake at front and rear.

Our first impression of the Cobra on the road was one of blinding acceleration in all gears. This was assisted considerably by the 3.77 axle ratio, and our feeling was that the car would be improved by a slightly lower numerical ratio because the engine is turning over unnecessarily fast at 70-75 mph cruising speeds. However, even with this ratio and using a peak of 7000 rpm, 60 mph can be achieved in 1st and a useful 100 mph in 3rd, and in consequence the passing ability of the car at any speed is nothing short of sensational. In traffic it is quite docile, although the clutch is heavy and considerable use must be made of the transmission.

Those people who are unaccustomed to driving cars with the potential of the Cobra would be advised to proceed with caution, because it is easy to find oneself going much too fast for comfort before one has realized what is happening. This does not mean that the car is particularly difficult to drive, because the tires and suspension do not permit excessive wheelspin off the line, unless one is very heavy handed, and shifting presents no problems at all. The main thing about it is that the Cobra reaches 100 mph while more conventional cars are struggling up to 75 mph, and this can be disconcerting to the uninitiated.

The AC Cobra is not just another sports car which someone has dumped a big V-8 into, but a properly conceived and developed machine which has been greatly improved by an extensive racing program. It offers exceptional performance without the problems of parts and service normally associated with cars of this nature. The AC Cobra is a sports car in the true sense of the term and, for those people who are not unduly concerned with comfort, it is a good value for the money.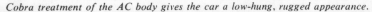

*Cobra treatment of the AC body gives the car a low-hung, rugged appearance.*

# FROM CARTS TO COBRAS
## HISTORY OF AC CARS

### BY DOUGLAS BLAIN

THE ORIGINAL BOSS of AC had the fine old British name of John Portwine, and he was a butcher by trade. He and designer/co-founder John Weller knew what the chopper was for when they set out building 3-wheel delivery trolleys back in 1904. Nut-hard business sense took the pair forward into proper car production with the perky little AC Sociable, pulled them head-high and hearty through four fierce years of war, and finally led them to sell out to dynamic, aristocratic race driver S. F. Edge at the height of their joint fame in 1922. The same wily worldliness underlies today's almost 18th century calm, setting AC Cars Limited right apart from its defiant but drastically depleted contemporaries.

You might rate the Cobra ample proof of the outfit's cash-and-carry philosophy. And you might suppose traditional standards of quality and inspection take a fourpenny fare at AC in the face of mid-century commercial consolidation. You'll be wrong with both guesses. Brother directors Charles and the late William Hurlock (they took over from Edge himself 33 years ago), with $1.5 million coming in from government contracts alone each year and a healthy machine-tool business lurking somewhere in the background, could give up car production tomorrow and still be joint kings of a castle bigger than Carroll Shelby or even FoMoCo could topple in a hurry. And the current AC Cobra, rolling at a leisurely 18 a week into Thames Ditton's peaceful market square, really does incorporate the priceless distillation of a

60-year-old tradition of construction for the custom trade.

The mighty Cobra, as Americans know it today, is a composite of this tailored tradition, with two external factors; specialized chassis design via competition development and transmogrified engine amortization through a bit of high-level hot-rodding. In fact, the world's fastest-accelerating production automobile incorporates a 10-year-old steel frame borrowed from the UK race track, a new-as-tomorrow powerplant adapted from an equally current American mass-assembly setup, a 9-year-old aluminum body shell derived from an even hoarier Italian couture original—all blended together by veteran craftsmen in a 59-year-old English factory for sale through a dynamic Texan Grand Prix driver (ret.) in partnership with the 50-year-old second-biggest manufacturer of basic transportation for the world.

Let's start with the frame. Essentially it's a stubby ladder structure of paired mild steel tubes—a singularly rugged, simple-looking blacksmith affair to eyes conditioned through roughly half a decade of intricate space and spaghetti.

Back in 1950, a relatively unknown named John Tojeiro evolved what was to become, could he only have seen it, the Cobra's sturdy heart. Toj's avowed idea (friends and fans alike still call him that) back then was to offer the amateur racing world a standard of road holding and a degree of engine variability which until that time must have seemed more than remote. These were to be all in a form and at a price that would put his brain child well within financial ⟫→

*Pugnacious styling is nothing new at AC; this is a 1923 AC, and a purposeful-looking machine it was.*

# AC FROM CARTS TO COBRAS

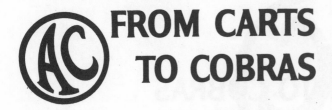

reach of the average enthusiast—even five years after a mighty tough war. In short, he was offering a package deal chassis, built by himself alone in a simple workshop at Bunt-ingford between London and Cambridge, for buyers to power and clothe however they thought fit.

An early customer was one Cliff Davis, a wild and florid-shirted character famed far and near for his peerless yearly parties, stentorian Cockney bellow and heart-stopping exper-tise at the wheel. Davis got Toj to install a highly modified Bristol six in place of the smaller type of powerplant usual in the chassis at that time. Result was a season so phenome-nally successful that fans still glow at the memory, even though neither Davis (he became a successful West London used car peddler) nor the Tojeiro-Bristol (it retired more or less to the club circuits) took any significant part in wheeled competition thereafter.

The Davis Tojeiro was the Cobra's root ancestor in more areas than one. Another item wild man Cliff ordered when he placed that so-significant first order was a special alumi-num body that would combine functionalism with a linear

beauty uncommon in British racing both then and now. Looking around for inspiration, designer Tojeiro found nothing of note in that particular direction at home. Instead, he turned to Italy. There Enzo Ferrari had just come up with what he hoped was the answer to Briton Syd Allard's domi-nation of the American big-inch market. To house the Lam-predi-designed mechanism of his new 200-hp, 4.1-liter Cad-crusher, Ferrari had Milan coachbuilder Carrozzeria Touring produce a modified version of the gracious shell that had formerly clad his smaller Mille Miglia 166 models of 1949—and it was this slightly altered 342 America skin that started off Tojeiro's English creation.

The America body by Touring was low and squat for its time, with little wasted panel area and no uncalled-for pro-jections. Focal points were a series of seams in the alloy paneling: one running across the nose above a rounded, rear-ward-sloping eggbox grille and then down under the lights at each side, another linking the tops of the wheel arches along each flank, a third dividing the hood and terminating in Ferrari's neat yellow badge at the forward lip. Twin frameless aero screens, heavily raked on a vertical painted-alloy base, shielded an oval leather-padded cockpit. Small hatch-like doors in the steeply chamfered sides eased pas-senger entry without interfering with Touring's well-known Superleggera principle of shaping all body openings for maxi-mum strength and framing them with narrow-gauge tubing as a rigid boundary for the semi-stressed metal skin. A tapered tail allowed marginal room for fuel and spare alone. In all it was a mean, weightless body, timeless and maybe

*Faded caption, circa 1924, reads, "My car as built . . ."*

*Four-seat tourer in 1933 had cycle fenders, polished alloy hood.*

*1937 AC sports roadster displayed lean lines and handsome good looks typical of AC design.*

even worthy of description as a peerless example of its kind.

Tojeiro's version was a pretty faithful nut and bolt copy. He narrowed the shell slightly to suit his frame dimensions, did away with the hard molding at waist level and took out the verticals from Ferrari's latticed snout. Lo! There, with one or two minor changes around cockpit and tail, was the UK 2-liter sports car leader of 1952.

And where does AC come in?

Postwar re-organization, stock-taking and general breath-getting found the Hurlock brothers' establishment at Thames Ditton in a fairly comfortable way. Munitions work had left the outfit with some useful extra factory space, cars were desperately short in Britain and materials for new ones hard to get. Shrewd businessmen that they were, the Hurlocks decided to go where the profit was and built biggish family sedans with just a trace of sports ancestry.

They started with an engine John Weller himself had designed during World War I and developed for production as early as 1919. It was no ordinary engine, no battered relic staggering in the wake of progress. His brain child was a 1.5-liter six at a time when the 6-cyl engine was regarded as a mechanical impossibility. It had not only overhead valves but a chain-driven overhead camshaft in a day when strong men winced at the thought of more than 2500 rpm on 4:1 compression. And most wonderful of all, it had a block, crankcase and sump structure cast entirely in aluminum, giving a total unit weight of 350 lb when the usual figure was anything up to three times as much.

This wonderful engine, a real milestone in automotive history, had served the little outfit well through 20 years of continuous production. "The First Light Six and Still the Finest," company engineers had boasted as they'd replaced the original iron head with an aluminum one, increased capacity to two liters, daringly pushed compression up from 4.75 to 5.25:1 and, hearts in mouths, finally added an extra bearing at the back of the crankshaft to make five in all and lay the bogey of what salesmen had been firmly instructed to refer to as "power throb."

For installation in the first postwar prototype (a hybrid with a prewar convertible body on a new underslung chassis), the Hurlocks specified a 70-bhp version of their beloved six with three SU carburetors feeding cast-in individual manifolds, 6:1 compression and, of course, the 5-bearing bottom end with wartime-perfected bronze and white metal shells. But foresight stopped at the engine. Torn between tradition and a half-expressed desire to keep up, the AC design team settled for a squat and frankly ugly ash-and-aluminum body that expressed neither adequately. Then they lumbered it with an uninspired chassis, non-independent leaf spring suspension and hydra-mechanical brakes. The new sedan (it never really had a name) sold a steady five a week and made the company a lot of money. Why? It was simple to produce by the old methods as well as reliable, roomy and—well, just a bit different in an age of sameness.

First sign of a return to the old AC sporting spirit came in 1950. Dreaming of a 4-place convertible companion to the well-established 2-liter, the Hurlocks arranged to have a trial batch built entirely outside on a chassis supplied from ⟫⟫→

*AC's "alloy six" was notable for clean looks, rugged construction.*

*Handsome engine was retained as hallmark of AC firm.*

*Below, left, is the Ferrari 166 Mille Miglia, with body by Carrozzeria Touring, which was the basis for Tojeiro's original body design. At right is the car AC directors saw when they approached John Tojeiro for a new design for their own car.*

Ace prototype built to Tojeiro's original design by AC; this car has bench seat, and weather protection has been added.

AC-Bristol variant designed by Tojeiro around special tube frame.

Early competition AC powered by Bristol engine.

Aceca coupe, now discontinued, used Ace parts.

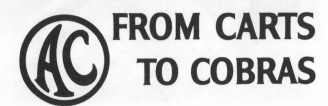

# FROM CARTS TO COBRAS

Thames Ditton. Most attractive tender for the intricate coachwork involved came from an outfit called Buckland Body Works Limited; the new soft-top—it got to be called the Buckland—was an instant success and the experiment became a regular contracted sideline. Even today a good Buckland will bring a fair price for its age, largely because the 4-place open body configuration has become such a rarity in Britain. But meanwhile a fast-rising enthusiast index in Britain's home and export markets led the Hurlocks to think of a genuine comeback in the 100 per cent sports car field. Like so many shrewd businessmen before them, they saw the wisdom of taking up an existing design rather than trying to catch up on 15 years of theory on their own. The point was, whose design?

Now it happened that Buckland Body Works lay just down the road from John Tojeiro at Buntingford, Hertfordshire. A visiting AC executive, in town to check on delivery of a new batch of convertibles, heard talk of the revolutionary race car taking shape in the neighborhood and came to have a look. Curiosity turned to intense interest when Toj pointed

out his frame's adaptability to any engine size within reason as well as its unique combination of production-oriented attributes; simplicity, low cost and technical currency. AC design chiefs set to work studying Tojeiro's blueprints with an eye to adapting his competition design for the highway. Toj himself discussed finance with the Hurlocks and their colleagues on the board. Finally everything seemed to dovetail. Tojeiro would get a lump sum for the body and chassis plans plus a royalty on sales up to a certain ceiling. Both parties would co-operate in developing the car for production. Weeks later a prototype appeared with similar bodywork to Cliff Davis' race winner, although it boasted a full-width glass windshield and a fully trimmed cockpit with split-bench padded seat.

The final Ace design, launched in 1954, used Toj's chassis with a few basic changes plus an updated version of his borrowed body design. Steering was by cam and lever instead of rack and pinion, and AC developed special hubs and kingpins as well as 16-in. wire wheels with offset rims for top stability. Michelin X tires were stock, largely because their sidewall flexibility suited the original suspension setup (transverse leaf springing usually means big wheel deflection angles, and the new car had it front and rear).

Body changes started in front, where lighting laws for road use in America meant higher headlamp mounts if AC was to export the cars as planned. Shifting the headlight centers up six inches changed the whole frontal styling, leaving room for sidelamps above the Ferrari-derived drooping lip and calling for a forward instead of a backward tilt to the

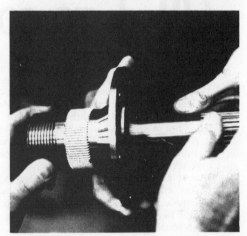

*Early Ace had drum brakes, cam and lever steering and AC's ohc engine.*　　　*Present rear hub, machined from forging.*

snout. It also meant that the original tail looked wrong, so AC's men gave it the delightful hump it still wears today and a lot of baggage space to boot. Minor alterations included restoring the vertical bars in the eggcrate grille, adding bumper overriders (but not bumpers) front and rear and specifying bucket seats in place of the prototype's bench. Net result was a car even better looking that Toj's original, less like a plagiarized Ferrari and more like the independent and highly original offering enthusiasts knew it to be.

One of the big reasons AC took on Tojeiro's design was that its universal character made installation of the ancient overhead-cam six a perfectly straightforward task. By now the veteran alloy powerplant was grinding out a regular 75 bhp, thanks to 6.5:1 compression and triple SU carburetors. For awhile it seemed AC had achieved the perfect marriage.

Soon, though, race ambitions on the part of one or two influential customers set the Hurlocks thinking of an optional competition power-pack. Rather than impose a straw that threatened to fracture their quarter-century-old camel's back (notwithstanding demonstrations to the contrary by one Ken Rudd, a race-minded dealer who boasted 105 hp from his still-reliable competition unit), they fixed on adapting an entirely new engine as a supplementary offering. Because tooling at Thames Ditton was minimal, old-fashioned and, of course, well and truly amortized already, and as installation of any new plant would have been uneconomic because of the factory's strictly limited output capacity, the decision really meant looking elsewhere for suitable material. Cliff Davis' beloved Bristol, now yielding a steady 120 bhp in

basic form as the power behind a heavy but interesting sedan, looked a mighty good bet. They tried it. It was.

A fine close-ratio 4-speed gearbox came with the Bristol unit as a package deal, eliminating the trusty but rather notchy Moss box (familiar to Americans in today's TR-powered Morgan) which still partnered the home-grown powerplant. The new engine became a catalogued Ace extra in D-2 tune, with 125 bhp at 5750 rpm on 9:1 compression and triple Solex downdraft carburetors. Its form is well-known: a beautifully finished in-line 2-liter six with a single camshaft mounted high in the block serving twin rocker arms via short pushrods and repeaters. The block was iron, the head aluminum and the nitrided crank in its four hefty bearings was statically and dynamically balanced before assembly. Bristol-powered cars soon began outselling the originals until AC was using more of the new engines than Bristol itself. The AC unit finally died an honorable death in 1960 after a whopping 27 years of continuous service and development—and still it had a lot of features modern competitors couldn't match!

Meanwhile, a slightly less powerful version of the Bristol plant appeared in a closed coupe called the Aceca, a truly beautiful automobile. The Aceca differed structurally from the Ace in that its supplementary tubular body frame contributed substantially to overall stiffness. Engine output was 105 bhp at lower revs, first gear had a freewheel for clutchless city shifting and overdrive was available on fourth. Like the coil-sprung, square-tube Greyhound coupe of 1959–61 (an unfortunate and short-lived mistake), the Aceca was

Cobra with detachable hardtop
ran at Le Mans in 1963.

Latest Cobra has special body
designed by Pete Brock (left).

# (AC) FROM CARTS TO COBRAS

outside the mainstream of Cobra background development
and needn't concern us too much. Production stopped in
1962. Also outside was the special space-frame car Tojeiro
designed for the factory to enter at Le Mans as a protoype
in 1958. It finished seventh overall, but the Hurlocks decided not to go ahead with a production version.

A good stock production Ace-Bristol would do over 90
in third gear and 115 in top; acceleration to 60 took just
over seven seconds and to 100 roughly 24—enough performance to guarantee for it the race success AC hoped for. Disc
brakes, offered as an option from 1956, made the car a real
proposition; in fact what with one thing and another AC
looked like riding high unless something unforeseen came
up to scupper the ship.

It did, too. At the end of 1959 Bristol Cars ran into
trouble that led to a break from the big aircraft outfit that
had spawned it just after the war. New boss George White
realized the only real way to cut costs was to scrap the firm's
intricate and highly expensive 6-cyl engine, by now too small
anyway for the newest product, and do a deal with Chrysler
of America for one of its Canadian-built V-8s. For AC that
meant it was time to look for something new, and quick.

This time the answer came from Ken Rudd, the man who
had pulled those extra ponies from the early overhead-cam
powerplant. Since its demise, dealer Rudd had taken to in-
flicting a private punishment called the Ruddspeed Conversion on Ford of Britain's unsuspecting 2.6-liter Zephyr six
and sliding the result under the Ace's ever-accommodating
hood either as a replacement for the original AC or Bristol
six or as original equipment in a bare chassis supplied from
Thames Ditton. His success encouraged the Hurlocks to try
the same idea, and pretty soon they were ready with a revised
model called the Ace 2.6—just in time, as it happened, for
the 1961 London Motor Show at Earl's Court.

Recognition features in the newcomer included a new
tapered nose and smaller grille plus slightly altered bumper
and weatherproofing arrangements. One significant mechanical change backed up the engine swap: disc brakes became
stock on the front wheels instead of an option as formerly.
A cunning sales ruse meant that the new cars left AC's
factory with completely unmodified Ford engines that went
directly to Rudd's establishment down the road at Worthing
where replacement units modified to give a healthy 140 bhp
lay waiting. The idea was that the customer paid UK purchase tax (at that time a crippling 50%) only on the stock
unit, even though it was hardly the thing for him to buy
his car without the Rudd proddings.

The ruse worked well enough in practice but, unfortunately, the engines didn't; comprehensive attention to the
Zephyr Mark III head put an unprecedented strain on the
bottom end, which usually held up within Rudd's prudent
redline limits but succumbed with heart-rending regularity
whenever an owner put much more than a toe over the edge.
Luckily, Ford of England came up with a new version of the
same unit to suit its thoroughly reworked Mark IV Zephyr/
Zodiac model range of mid-1962—and the changes included
extra strengthening for crankshaft, main journals and big-
ends. One or two of the revised powerplants found their way
into 2.6 Aces and showed every sign of yielding yeoman
service, but in the meantime yet another quiet revolution
had gripped the tiny factory.

AC's new harbinger of total re-orientation was tall, Texan
and (to any modest Briton) more than a little terrifying. He
dropped in one day to announce his arrival in England on a
shopping expedition for an established competition-bred
European automobile capable of accepting a correspondingly familiar American V-8, for sale to the U.S. public and possible 50-50 usage on highway and race track. You-all down
here in li'l ole Thames Ditton, opined the bronzed grand
prix veteran with a window-rattling business chuckle, looked
from Stateside to have about the right kind of setup and—
well, here he was.

Nobody could deny the cold logic underlying Shelby's
Southern drawl, and the Hurlocks, for all their inborn British
reticence, were hardly the men to let ceremony stand in the
way of sales. The Texan, it seemed, was in business to sell
cars and U.S. sales were what AC had long been counting
on. If Ford's V-8 would fill the hole lately vacated by Bristol's
six and currently held on short-term tenancy by Ford of
England's ditto, then no doubt AC's development boys could
make whatever resulted into an acceptable dual-purpose sales
proposition.

Actually, Shelby proved to have ideas in that quarter, too.
His homework had been more thorough than he'd indicated
at first, and before the little factory really managed to grasp
what it was in for, the one-time toast of two continents
(Shelby's racing record is as well remembered in Europe as at
home) had produced rough drawings and a full week's worth
of verbal instructions to cover almost every detail of the
scheme he had in mind.

But eventually, like the good fairy in all the best kids'
stories, he flew away into the west and left AC to get down to
the serious business of building and developing a prototype.
Paperwork and consultations with well-known designers and
stress engineers showed that most of the original Tojeiro
frame should stand up under what would amount to a 300%
maximum twist stress increase coupled with a significant
weight jump, although the metal used for the twin ladder
tubes and for the hooped steel scuttle and front roll-bar
structure would need to be upped at least one gage. Thicker
mild steel sheet for the support boxes at each end of the
frame would take care of much-multiplied-lateral stresses at

# FROM CARTS TO COBRAS

the wheels, and a supplementary cage of tubes around the rubber-mounted final drive would help distribute strain from the Ford's tremendous shaft torque.

Running gear would need to be almost doubled in breaking strain: Shelby had already fixed on Borg-Warner's alloy-cased 4-speed, all-synchro gearbox (a listed Ford option) as basic equipment and to match it AC chose the heaviest possible Hardy Spicer propshaft, universals (six of 'em) and rear wheel driveshafts. Salisbury had just announced a UK-built PowrLok limited-slip differential, so the Hurlocks ordered the version originally developed for Jaguar's Mark X and specified certain exterior and ratio changes to suit their new application. Together with strengthened suspensions, giant outboard disc brakes for the back wheels as well as the front and special hubs and stub-axles machined and hardened at Thames Ditton to a new specification, these important but hardly fundamental changes looked capable of adapting Toj's 10-year-old design quite adequately for its new role on U.S. tracks and turnpikes.

So the Hurlocks thought, anyway, as they crated that first prototype for shipment to Shelby's new testing, development and assembly plant. A few weeks later came the first reports of trouble. Despite the experts' predictions, the slow-churning Ford was chewing out the new car's rear hubs. Worse, road holding was well below par and Shelby's drivers were having trouble laying the engine's power on the road even when they could get it as far as the wheels. Both sides had ideas about a cure. While AC techniques concentrated on strengthening the rear frame cage still further, on developing a revised and even stronger driving hub and on building five more prototypes for shipment without engines, Shelby busied himself with ideas for spoking-out the original wire wheels and fitting bigger U.S.-built low-profile tires for better stability and traction. This period also brought the final version of the Cobra body shape, with the smaller grille developed for the Ace 2.6 in combination with a characteristic lip around all wheel openings—adopted, of course, to clear the enormous wheels Shelby's experiments dictated. Internal changes included a fiberglass firewall sheathing pigmented in white to reflect heat from the V-8's exhaust, plus a new tail layout incorporating an outsize fuel tank mounted directly over the final drive instead of in the fender. The spare tire moved from its old location inside the luggage compartment to a fiberglass tray under the trunk floor.

After selected U.S. magazines had wowed their readers with highly favorable reports on the prototypes submitted to them for test, and after Shelby himself had made sure of a competition future for the car and laid the basis for his now-famous circuit team, AC got the word to lay down an initial 100-car run of production Cobras for sale to American consumers. After this first batch came the swing to Ford's hot, 300-bhp V-8 (formerly an option) in place of the original 260, followed a little later by the offer of a fiberglass hardtop based on the one AC had offered with its Bristol-powered Ace. Minor identification points for later-type Cobras included tubular double bumpers to supplement the original outsize overriders front and rear and a tiny Powered-By-Ford flash in anodized aluminum on each flank near the door.

Cobra production today is concentrated almost wholly in the compact but surprisingly well-equipped AC plant at Thames Ditton. The cars leave England built-up, fully painted and complete except for engines, gearboxes and a few minor details such as speedo and tach. The long (about four weeks' work for every car) and intricate (several hundred distinct processes in roughly a dozen "shops" or departments) routine starts in AC's own tube-bending department, where skilled operators cut and bend the lengths of cold-drawn mild steel tube required for building both the simple basic chassis and the complex semi-triangulated subframe that supports the body panels. Bending is done without heat and without any spring or sand insert in a series of crude but highly effective wooden hand-presses. After it has settled to its new shape the tubing passes to a corner of AC's machine shop, where a special cutter shapes the radiused ends for welding.

Welding itself is the first true production-line process. Highly trained craftsmen take the pre-shaped tubes and steel sheets and assemble them on special jigs, tack-welding the key joints first and then following up with a more permanent bond. Each complete frame weighs under 200 lb.

The underbody is an inner skin in uncontoured aluminum and molded fiberglass sheet forming fender skirts, underhood splash panels, floor—for which AC uses a much thicker gage aluminum—dash, trunk lining and battery and tire wells. The body itself is hand-made and fitted elsewhere; trucks arrive daily with the finished shells and take away new chassis to be clothed in the cramped and furiously busy North London contractor's plant (it's actually a converted railroad station) that has built AC's bodies since 1935. The intricately contoured panels are not actually beaten with hammers: they're rolled out in small sections on a weird-looking device called a wheeling machine and then welded together into manageable sizes on a full-scale wood and fiberglass Cobra mockup. After a little manual adjustment to guarantee perfect fit they're finally riveted to the frame and shipped back to the main plant for painting.

And painting a Cobra body isn't the simple mechanical process you might have in mind. First step is to brush up the welded joints where small working panels became bigger replacement units; wire brushing levels the weld and makes the area take better. Next comes an etching coat designed to eat the surface polish off the aluminum and bed into the metal itself. Five coats of thick gray filler follow, smoothing out detail imperfections and building up a crack-resistant layer for the pigment. A special sealer neutralizes the filler, its color chosen to highlight the shade of the finishing coat: for example, a red car gets a brilliant pink sealer to give it depth and individuality. Final pigment goes on in four or five coats depending on color, each one again hand-rubbed, and the whole car gets a top layer of thick wax polish to protect it during shipment. Drying, thanks to the Cobra's advent, is now an artificial process although AC retained a natural drying room until a year ago.

Complete standardization has meant the end, too, for a long-standing AC tradition of customer participation. The slow pace of things up to 1962 gave the Ace buyer (or his wife) a chance not only to choose the exact color for his car, but to supervise its actual application. Sales manager Henderson even has a stock joke about a wife who was so horrified at seeing the decrepit wheels factory workers had used for pushing hubby's car around the paint plant that she insisted on returning later to make sure they were replaced! But today there's none of that. Shelby sends his color orders through in batches of five and AC complies without question.

After paint comes trim, and there again AC relies on craftsmen with their priceless, time-consuming individual skills. Hides arrive, still cow-shaped, from top-quality supplier

CONTINUED ON PAGE 55

# RACE TUNING THE FORD-COBRA

**BY TONY HOGG**

A RECENT ANNOUNCEMENT from Shelby American served notice the Cobra team will be contesting in the 1964 series of classic European road races which count toward the international manufacturer's championship. These events include the LeMans 24-hour race, the Nurburgring 1000 Kilometers, and the Targa Florio in Sicily among others and, of course, our own Sebring 12-hour event which was run last March and resulted in a 1-2-3 class victory for the Shelby team.

The Cobras are "Powered by Ford," and with this in mind we made a recent visit to the Cobra plant in Venice, Calif., and followed it up with a trip to Sebring with the team in order to find out exactly how the 289-cu. in. Ford engine is prepared for long distance sports car events, and how it withstands this sort of treatment.

The demands of road racing are remarkably varied and depend largely on

the length of the particular race and the nature of the circuit. The length of the race may be anywhere from a one-hour sprint event to the 24 hours of LeMans; the circuit may be short, twisty and slow, or long and fast, or possibly even a combination of the two. For this reason, it is normal practice to set up an engine for a specific race and, in the case of teams such as Cobra, to enter several cars with different power characteristics so that a balance is achieved between speed and reliability.

For this reason, ultimate horsepower is not always the most important consideration. The stress lies more upon the torque curve. However, normal horsepower figures for the competition Cobra engines lie between 340 and 370 depending on specific conditions, but the aim is to concentrate the power output between 4500 rpm and 6500 rpm, although a peak of 7200 rpm can

be used if necessary. On the circuits which incorporate a long straight it seems to be advantageous to gear the car so that the normal rev range is used, with a peak of 7200 rpm reached just at the braking point on the straight. In the same way that brake horsepower is not a prime consideration, the speed of the car in miles per hour is disregarded and the important thing is the engine revolutions at particular points on the circuit and, of course, the lap times. In fact, a competition Cobra will reach about 165 mph on a circuit incorporating a sufficiently long straight.

The Cobra engines start life as the production line 271-bhp version of the Ford 289-cu. in. unit and they are received at the Cobra shop in the same condition as when they are shipped to the various Ford assembly plants. Although the stock 289s are exceptionally well designed and precisely con-

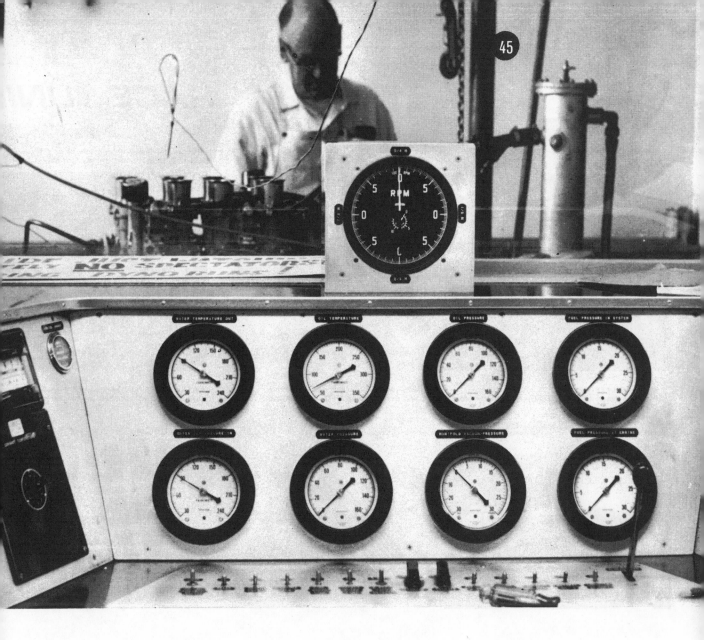

structed engines, Cobra competition engine builders Cecil Bowman and Jack Hoare look upon them as a set of rough castings to be worked up into a racing engine.

Perhaps the most surprising thing about the Cobra engines is the number of stock parts that are used and also how little the finished product really varies from the original Ford power unit. In fact, one very soon finds out that it is the extremely precise assembly and attention to detail which wins races rather than any very radical modifications. And it is evident that detail work is the secret to the Cobra's success.

The first procedure is to strip the engine to the last nut and bolt. Then the standard bores are honed out to racing clearances of at least 0.006 in. The stock pistons and rings are used, with a ring gap of 0.018 in. A considerable amount of time is spent on the

heads and the major modification is the fitting of 1/16 in. larger valves. This increases the diameter of the intakes to 1.875 in. and the exhausts to 1.625 in. To take advantage of the larger valves, the ports are opened up, and finally the combustion chambers are machine-polished. The next step is to mill the heads to obtain the desired compression ratio, but before milling it is necessary to weld the surface of the head at one point to strengthen the water jacket.

As far as compression is concerned, a ratio in the region of 11.6:1 is normally used, although engines have been raced with ratios as high as 12.5. In order to obtain 11.6, it is necessary to mill about 0.040 in. from the heads because quite a lot of metal has to be removed from the combustion chambers to obtain the desired finish. To insure that the compression ratio is correct and that the capacity of each

combustion chamber is the same, each chamber is measured with the piston at top dead center by filling it with fluid from a calibrated container.

Although the stock crankshaft and connecting rods are retained, the manufacturer's balance is not fine enough for racing standards so the shaft is rebalanced with the damper and clutch assembly as a unit. The oil feed holes to the journals are relieved slightly. The journals themselves are polished with crocus cloth and finished with jeweler's rouge. The engine bearings are Clevite bronze T-77 material.

The oil capacity is increased to 8 qt. by welding on additions to the sides of the existing oil pan and the pan is then cadmium-plated to prevent corrosion from acid. An oil cooler is mounted in front of the radiator, although these were relocated on the Sebring cars when temperatures as high as 260° were reached during practice. The

**RACE-READY** heads show evidence of extensive polishing, larger valves, milled surface.

**HIGH-PERFORMANCE** Ford 289 engines are treated as rough castings, get reworked.

**CAST ROCKER** covers add distinctive and decorative appearance to engine.

**SOLID LIFTERS,** stiff springs and keepers from valve train; camshaft is little changed.

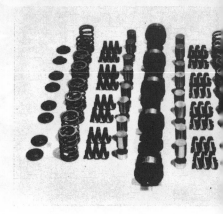

stock oil pump is retained but the clearances are checked carefully and the spring tension of the pressure relief valve is increased. Because of the resulting increase in oil pressure, the oil supply to the rockers is reduced. This prevents an over-accumulation of oil in the rocker covers when the engines are run constantly in the 4000-7000 rpm range. At the same time the oil pan capacity is increased, the baffling is rearranged and the oil pickup pipe and screen are reinforced; this overcomes surge and starvation problems which may be induced by violent maneuvering.

During most of 1963, which was the first season of active participation in racing for the Cobra team, the stock 271-bhp camshaft of the 289 engine was used. The result was an excessively wide torque curve, making the cars reliable and relatively easy to drive on any circuit but at the sacrifice of maximum power output. Therefore, a variety of different grinds based on the stock cam have been tried recently, al-

though they have all been fairly conservative in order to keep the torque curve within reasonable limits. However, the valve train in the 289 engine is the limiting factor and although 7200 rpm is a safe rev limit it can quickly lead to failure if used with any kind of a wild cam grind.

When setting up an engine for a particular race and circuit, the ignition timing and advance curve together with the carburetion have to be considered in conjunction with the camshaft. The vacuum advance to the distributor is disconnected and the advance curve is adjusted by using springs of various strengths to obtain the desired curve. Depending on the particular engine, the static advance is between 8 and 12° and the total advance between 34 and 40° at 5000 rpm.

As far as carburetion is concerned, the Cobra competition engine uses four twin-throat downdraft Italian Webers, which are practically mandatory for winning road races in this

day and age. The Weber is an extremely expensive instrument and a complete set of four with manifold suitable for the 289 engine can be bought from Shelby American for $1230; however, they are not recommended for street use.

The Weber is not a progressive type of carburetor, because both throttles open simultaneously, and there is no connection between the two chokes other than a common fuel supply system. Therefore, when four Webers are fitted to an 8-cyl. engine, individual carburetion is provided for each cylinder. When this is matched to the Cobra's scientifically designed exhaust system, which has been developed from dynamometer tests with various layouts, the results are extremely effective.

The main characteristic of the Weber is that all the components which affect performance are almost infinitely variable, so that one can build up a carburetor practically from scratch to suit any particular circumstance. How-

# THE FORD COBRA

**LIGHTWEIGHT headers extract exhaust into collectors and huge tail pipes.**

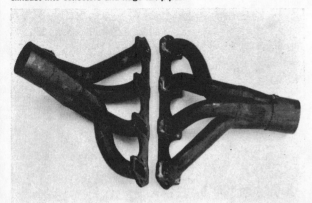

**FIRST IN GT class and 4th overall at past Sebring was this aerodynamic coupe-bodied Cobra.**

**WEBER INTAKE system, at $1230 per, is essential for racing but hardly suitable for the street.**

**PAYOFF FOR the painstaking precision comes at the race course, where Cobras now harry Ferraris and submerge Sting Rays.**

ever, this presupposes a considerable amount of experience with Webers and also with the characteristics of the particular engine. It is also necessary to have a supply of the various sizes of jets and other parts to be interchanged.

One of the rules governing sports car racing requires the engine to be stopped during a pit stop and then restarted by its own starter motor. Furthermore, a part of the long-distance events like LeMans and Sebring are run at night, so it is essential to have a reliable electrical system. For this reason, the Cobras are equipped with alternators and particular attention is paid to the charging circuit. In addition, heavy-duty starters are fitted because a racing engine equipped with Webers can be difficult to start when either hot or cold; the diameter of the venturis is too big to create much of a vacuum at cranking speeds.

In its bid for honors in European sports car racing, the Cobra team will be opposed by Ferrari, which has won the championship for the last three years and has a formidable background in road racing. Ferrari will be entering a team of highly specialized cars powered by V-12 overhead camshaft engines of 242 cu. in. coupled to 5-speed transmissions, which will be extremely hard to beat. However, it is generally considered that the Cobras do have a good chance and, should they be successful, it will prove that the Ford 289 engine, using stock components and meticulous assembly, is at least the equal of any engine in the world.

A comparison between the Ferraris and the Cobras shows that the Cobras have the edge in some respects, but the Ferraris are probably the best all around competition cars. The Ferrari engine is reputed to put out 370 bhp at 7200 rpm. Its usable power range is much narrower than that of the Cobras, but the Ferrari 5-speed transmission compensates in part for this deficiency. However, it is in the all-important area of road-holding that the Ferraris have the edge, because the Cobras are relying on the basic English

AC chassis which is at best a 10-year-old design.

During practice for the Sebring event, the best Ferrari lap time was 3 min., 4.2 sec., while the Cobras were unable to get below 3 min. 12.8 sec. The reason for the difference was road-holding rather than any lack of engine power. In the 12-hour race itself, the overall winning Ferrari covered 214 laps of the 5.2-mile circuit and the best placed Cobra 209 laps. And, although the Ferraris placed 1-2-3, the Cobras were fourth, fifth and sixth.

The most interesting contest will be the 24-hour race at LeMans on June 20. In the 1963 event, the winning Ferrari averaged 118 mph for the race, with a fast lap of 128 mph, and was clocked at 180 mph over a section of the Mulsanne straight. For this race the Cobra team will be relying on the more aerodynamic coupe version of the car, which should be able to attain equal speeds. But whether they will be able to do so for a period of 24 hours remains to be seen. ∎

# Cobra Sports Roadster

## Who Can Put a Price on Sheer Fun?

EVERY MANUFACTURER of a jazzed-up hardtop who thinks his car is a genuine "sports car," should be required to take a test hop in one of the Ford powered Shelby AC Cobras. To say that he would be enlightened is understatement—more likely he would be terrified as well as edified.

The Cobra is so unlike other cars on the market today that that test-driving manufacturer certainly would not recognize many features which it and his own product would have in common. Thus, when the Cobra is doing what it can do best, it is so far removed from the pres-

ent automotive concepts and standards as to be a completely unfamiliar entity. It represents, we think, the far, far-out end of the automotive spectrum.

In the first place, the AC Cobra is more than a mere car; it is a collection of ideas organized into the age-old concept that an auto ought to do what its human master bids, that it ought to be fun to drive, and that it ought to be an extension of the driver's hands, feet and senses. It was never intended to be mere transportation for two people from Point A to Point B. It was designed to give the driver pleasure over every foot of road.

By U.S. manufacturers' standards, however, the Cobra would be crude, uncomfortable, noisy, costly, harsh, jiggly, breezy and totally unacceptable. Few people, he would argue, would be willing to put up with such annoyances, just for the masochistic thrill or two. His argument is no doubt correct and there undoubtedly are only a few (thousand) people willing to put up with those things in order to accept the AC Cobra for what it is—an out-and-out, red-blooded, ground-hugging, road-eating sports car.

Fortunately enough for Carroll Shelby, AC Cars Ltd. of England and the Ford Motor Company, these people are standing in a line that extends from Shelby-American's Venice, Calif., snake-pit all the way back past the bank. The supply of cars just can't seem to catch up to the demand, even at the asking price of $5995 (before extras). The market, such as it is, no doubt is very small in terms of hundreds and thousands of units, but it is perhaps one of the most interesting phenomena of this manufacturing era. It is perhaps significant that this type of car can be built (assembled) and sold, profitably, by the coalition of efforts from two small companies and one very big one.

Hopefully, this sort of thing could lead into some more high-performance, high-style, low-production cars. There are several other examples around already, such as the Apollo GT, which combines an Italian-built body with the small Buick V-8 engine and suspension components; the Iso-Rivolta, of similar origins but with Chevrolet V-8 power; and, the Sunbeam "Street Tiger," a smaller English sports car with the 260-cu. in. version of Ford Fairlane V-8. Several other English cars (not imported) are also making use of big-inch American V-8s for power, notably the Bristol and the Jensen (Chrysler).

The whole idea of mating a powerful American engine to a lighter, more maneuverable European body is not very new. Sydney Allard was doing it in England with flathead Fords and Mercs 20 years ago and, as a result, achieving considerable success in hill-climbs and road races. Somewhat later, the French Facel-Vega utilized the 361-cu. in. Chrysler V-8s for propulsion of several notably-quick *Gran Turismo* sedans. In fact,

we might trace the idea back to the halcyon days of hot rodding, when it was *de rigueur* to stuff a warmed-up flat-head V-8 between the skimpy frame rails of a Model T or A Ford.

It might be well to equate the AC Cobra in terms of the ubiquitous hot rod, since this is a term better understood, perhaps, than sports car. As we've said, it follows the typical hot rod pattern of having a "big" engine in a light-weight, whippy chassis. The engine is super-tuned to deliver a far greater-than-ordinary amount of power. But, here is where the Cobra, and most other sports cars, differ from the hot rod. The Cobra's chassis is such that it matches, in capabilities, the performance of the drivetrain. In other words, the Cobra has a great deal of inherent cornering ability, stopping ability and maneuverability.

The Cobra's chassis is a long distillation of traditional English road racing design dating back to the early '20s. Although it stems more directly from the Ace sports roadster designed for AC Cars Ltd. by one John Tojeiro more than 12 years back, it has been updated to the point where it at least has reasonably modern attributes.

The basis for the design is a pair of longitudinal mild-steel tubes that end in lateral box-section crossmembers which carry the front and rear suspensions. With a few more crossmembers thrown in to support engine and transmission, and to provide torsional stiffness, this follows the well-known ladder frame pattern that, at the time of its design in 1950–52, was standard racing car practice (but which has subsequently been replaced by space frame and monocoque body/chassis systems). A large-diameter steel tube forms a hoop

at the cowl to support the front of the body and another tubular support carries the load at the rear. The body itself, made of rolled out, not hammer-stretched, aluminum panels, has a supporting substructure which attaches to these main braces and the frame, making it in all a reasonably rigid chassis/body.

The suspension consists of lower A-frame arms and transverse leaf springs, front and rear. Although simple in concept, design and construction, this independent front and rear system still does not provide the optimum in road-holding because of the parallelogram movement it imparts to the wheels. However, it is fully independent, and the advantages (over live axles, for instance) far outweigh any disadvantages. The leaf springs are mounted atop the terminal structures and form the upper control arms for the hub-carriers. The carriers' lower ends are pivoted to the outboard end of the A-arms (the apex of the A). Shock absorbers attach at the lower arms and to the box-structure. Steering is a positive rack-and-pinion system, which needs only 2.75 turns of the steering wheel to move the front wheels from left to right lock.

An independent rear suspension requires an articulated drive system and the AC Cobra is a good example of what can be done with existing components. While AC machines its own hub-carriers (a part of the AC organization is a very large and profitable machine-shop business), it buys six large universal joints, two half-shafts and one propeller shaft from Hardy-Spicer for each car. The differential is made by Salisbury and is similar to the one used by Jaguar of England for its big Mark X sedans. The differential is mounted di-

# Cobra Roadster

rectly to the frame and is driven by the single, short shaft from the transmission. The power is taken out to the wheels on the half-shafts, which have universal joints at each end. All driving, braking and cornering loads are transmitted to the frame by the wide-based lower arms and upper spring/arm. Thus, unsprung weight is kept reasonably low (the lower arms are welded up of steel tubing) and the rear roll center kept to an acceptable height above the ground. Rear wheels of the Cobra are decambered about 2° to further improve cornering ability and traction, something possible only with an i.r.s.

It should be mentioned that the brakes are of the disc type, mounted in the usual inside-the-wheel position. The actual discs are machined by AC, but the calipers and other hydraulic equipment are supplied by Girling of England (which also supplied the design that Bendix manufactures under license in this country for use on Studebakers). Although discs are still a novelty in this land of the quick-fade drum brakes, AC has been putting discs on its cars since 1956!

In its salad days, the AC Ace, from whence the Cobra version sprang, (or should we say struck?) was a highly regarded sports car, capable of acquitting itself equally well on road or track. Competing against cars with less sophisticated suspensions and brakes, it had little trouble in outrunning them, par-

ticularly in the under-2-liter class where its 6-cyl. engines placed it. Light weight was also one of its virtues and an Ace-Bristol (Bristol 6-cyl. engine, 145 bhp) could scale less than 1800 lb. when readied for the race. Small wonder then that when retired road racing driver Carroll Shelby was casting about for a suitable chassis for his proposed sports car he took a good, strong look at the AC Ace, among others.

Shelby, a Texan, achieved a good deal of fame both in the U.S. and abroad for his feats in both sports car and Grand Prix car racing. A seemingly happy-go-lucky sort, Shelby nonetheless knew what he wanted, and generally got it. When he retired from competitive racing in '61 he sought a way to manufacture his own sort of automobile. Like others, Shelby had figured that the combination of the big American V-8 in a roadable, stylish European chassis was just the sort of expensive thing he could sell in limited quantities in the U.S.

A preliminary deal between an Italian coach-builder, Shelby and Chevrolet fell through—for various reasons. Then, Shelby had a scheme to build his cars in Mexico, but government approval and/or financial backing fell through on this one. Somewhat later, Shelby stirred the interest of the Ford Motor Company, which just happened to be looking for an image-maker to compete with Chevrolet's Corvette. Ford had also just announced its Fairlane series of "senior"

compact cars and had as part of the lineup a pair of lightweight ohv V-8s. Ford engineers, too, were pretty high on the possibilities for developing really impressive amounts of horsepower from this design. So, when Shelby's search went to England, he was armed with a 260 bhp, 260-cu. in. Ford V-8 power-plant. Ford had agreed to supply the engines.

At Thames Ditton, Shelby's arrival was apocalyptic. It coincided with AC's almost-retirement from the sports car field. The firm's own 6-cyl. engine had long been outdated and its supply of Bristol 6-cyl. engines had been cut off by that firm's decision to drop its manufacture of this particular unit. Experiments with English Ford 6-cyl. engines had not yielded the desired reliability and AC, until Shelby came along, was faced with the fact that it had a good sports car chassis, but no suitable engine.

The marriage was a natural. By increasing frame tubing thickness by one gauge, the chassis was made husky enough. By using the strongest available U-joints and differential, most of the drive problems were solved. Redesigning the hub-carriers solved another. The short, compact Ford V-8 fell into place like a penny in a gum machine. AC Cobra was in business.

Several other problems arose, however, as Shelby took the cars into a competitive program designed to put the name into the forefront of sportscardom. One was that the cars needed to handle better, and two, they needed to go faster in order to be able to thrash Corvettes and Ferraris in production-class events. The first problem was taken care of by Shelby's insistence that they be shod with wide-rim 72-spoke wire wheels and Goodyear racing tires. The second prob-

**LEATHER UPHOLSTERY, wood-rimmed wheel and businesslike instruments give the Cobra cockpit a purposeful look.**

**POWERED BY FORD means, in this instance, 271 bhp and a 7000 rpm redline, and all the performance a man can use!**

lem was a little harder, but when Ford went to 289 cu. in. with the Fairlane V-8 in 1963, the standard power jumped from 260 to 271 bhp. More important, the base for the optional racing engine was improved and this unit, with its quadruple dual-throat Weber Carburetors, produces well over 330 bhp. ("Race-Tuning the Ford Cobra," July CL).

The normal Cobra engine is Ford's production-line High Performance 289-cu. in. V-8, rated 271 bhp at 6000 rpm, and 312 lb.-ft. torque at 3400 rpm. This engine is optional for Ford Fairlanes and Falcons, and Mercury's Comet, at a premium of nearly $500 over the standard 289 list price. Key to the HP-289's development of more, and stronger, horses is the use of cylinder heads with bigger ports and valves, a higher-lift camshaft, mechanical lifters, 11.6:1 compression and exhaust headers.

Valve size is 1.670 in. intake, 1.450 exhaust; lift is 0.477 in. and timing is 44-82-92-34, where the normal 289/195 bhp has specifications of 1.670, 1.389, 0.368 and 20-66-56-20, and a compression ratio of only 8.7:1. It's pretty easy to see that a good deal of the Cobra's venom comes from healthy engine breathing characteristics. Although the power peak is at 6000 rpm, it is easily possible to see 7000 rpm on the mechanical tachometer, and indeed, it doesn't seem to get any valve bounce until at least this point. For the test purposes, however, conservative 6800 rpm shift points were used, as these seemed to give best all-around acceleration.

The block, of course, is Ford's thin-wall V-8, with its ultra-short stroke of 2.87 in. and 2.248 in. diameter main bearings. For the 271-bhp engine, Ford uses a slightly stronger crankshaft and tougher bearing material than it does

with the normal 289/195 bhp. There are no other changes, except at the flywheel and clutch where Ford specifies a Long semi-centrifugal clutch of 1585 lb. pressure rather than the normal 1269-lb. unit. The 4-speed transmission used in the Cobra is the Warner Gear T-10 which has more than enough torque capacity for this engine. Its excellent synchronization and easy shifting help make the Cobra a pleasure to drive.

The overall gear ratio supplied with the Cobra is 3.77:1 which gives, at 6800 rpm, a top speed of 133 mph—far more than most drivers can ever utilize. A 3.54:1 was first tried in the prototype car, and is still used for some racing circuits, but it gave the Cobra a top of more than 150! So, the Shelby American people figured it was better to let the engine scream a little than to have all that top end potential. A 4.11:1 gearset is available on special order, for the more competitive-minded.

In traditional English sports car style, the Cobra is finished with a genuine leather interior, comfortable hip-hugging bucket seats and a wood-rimmed steering wheel. The floor is carpeted, the dash is full of functional, simple, informative Stewart-Warner instruments (even one for oil temperature). But there is not one ounce of frippery; it is all designed to do something or tell something. How refreshing!

Weather protection is minimal and lightweight. A simple, hand-erected canvas top stretches over tubular bows and clamps to the windshield header. Side-curtains lift out and are stored in a leather pocket behind the seats. High speed with the top up produces drafts and flaps, but then one could argue that the Cobra is a car designed to be driven with the top down. An optional hardtop

is available for those who desire more comfort in the cooler climes.

Driving the Cobra is best described as pure fun. It can also be described as "invigorating," "astounding," and "terrifying." The Cobra is obviously a driver's car and the more skilled a driver he is, the more he will enjoy it. Perversely, it doesn't really take a talented driver to drive the car. The engine is so docile at lower rpms, the transmission is so easy to use (it can be driven in only second and fourth gears if the driver is lazy), and the directional stability so good that any well-coordinated human being of reasonable acumen can safely operate and enjoy it.

The other side of the coin is that the Cobra can do things so quickly—accelerate, corner, brake, dart in and out of traffic holes—that its image can be easily and brutally abased by the inconsiderate driver. And, the inexperienced driver could quickly get into trouble 'way over his head if he lacks the prudence to "shut off." For instance, the acceleration from 40 to 80 mph, takes as little as 5 sec., a span short enough that the unmindful driver can easily over run any traffic in front of him, just from trying to pass too quickly.

Cornering abilities are astounding, even though the suspension tends to tip the tires the wrong way when the car leans into a curve. The wide, low Goodyear G8s, an outgrowth of that firm's stock and sports car racing tire development, really do the job of providing a good, fully controllable, slip angle. By virtue of its slight rearward weight bias, the Cobra has a slight oversteering tendency. This can be used to advantage in tight cornering as the powerful engine helps boost the rear around in a slightly wider arc than the front wheels and the

**FUEL TANK** fits into space over differential, thus leaving surprisingly large luggage room. Tank capacity is 18 gal.

**TOP DOWN,** or top up, the Cobra is a handsome hunk of car! Tires are low-profile, 7.35-15 Goodyear G8s, really hold the road.

# Cobra Roadster

whole action, properly controlled, makes for a great feeling of nimbleness.

Crooked roads, then, become challenges, and freeways increasingly dull. The Cobra is a go-fast car; the sort of car that makes its driver feel he could have taken that last corner at least 40 mph faster. And, he probably could have, too. The Cobra's abilities are such that maximum cornering speeds are beyond the comprehension of normal drivers. This same thing applies to the car's acceleration—it is so fierce that it can hypnotize the unaccustomed.

What price this glory? Shelby American lists the car at $5995 and has a list of optional dress-up items (our test car had Group A, which brought the total to $6343) and competition equipment, none of which are necessary to get the full enjoyment of the car. Is it worth the price of a Lincoln, an Imperial or Cadillac? Probably not in terms of comfort, durability and carrying capacity, but who could ever put a cost figure on fun? And who can evaluate the satisfaction of looking back over a crookedy road and thinking, "Boy, I took those pretty well!" ∎

## CAR LIFE ROAD TEST

### 1964 AC COBRA
### Sports Roadster

### SPECIFICATIONS

| | |
|---|---|
| List price | $5995 |
| Price, as tested | 6343 |
| Curb weight, lb | 2206 |
| Test weight | 2546 |
| distribution, % | 47/53 |
| Tire size | 7.35-15 |
| Tire capacity, lb | n.a. |
| Brake swept area | est. 580 |
| Engine type | V-8, ohv |
| Bore & stroke | 4.00 x 2.87 |
| Displacement, cu. in. | 288.5 |
| Compression ratio | 11.6 |
| Carburetion | 1 x 4 |
| Bhp @ rpm | 271 @ 6000 |
| equivalent mph | 117 |
| Torque, lb-ft | 314 @ 3400 |
| equivalent mph | 62 |

### EXTRA-COST OPTIONS

Grille guard, wsw tires, sun visors, windwings, heater, seat belts, chrome engine accessories, luggage rack.

### DIMENSIONS

| | |
|---|---|
| Wheelbase, in | 90.0 |
| Tread, f &,r | 51.5/52.5 |
| Overall length, in | 151.5 |
| width | 61.0 |
| height | 49.0 |
| equivalent vol, cu. ft | 262 |
| Frontal area, sq. ft | 16.6 |
| Ground clearance, in | 5.0 |
| Steering ratio, o/a | n.a. |
| turns, lock to lock | 2.75 |
| turning circle, ft | 34 |
| Hip room, front | 2 x 16.5 |
| Hip room, rear | n.a. |
| Pedal to seat back, max | 41.0 |
| Floor to ground | 10.5 |
| Luggage vol, cu. ft | 5.5 |
| Fuel tank capacity, gal | 18.0 |

### GEAR RATIOS

| | |
|---|---|
| 4th (1.00) overall | 3.77 |
| 3rd (1.41) | 5.32 |
| 2nd (1.78) | 6.71 |
| 1st (2.36) | 8.90 |

### CALCULATED DATA

| | |
|---|---|
| Lb/hp (test wt) | 9.4 |
| Cu. ft/ton mile | 170 |
| Mph/1000 rpm | 19.5 |
| Engine revs/mile | 3070 |
| Piston travel, ft/mile | 1470 |
| Car Life wear index | 45.2 |

### SPEEDOMETER ERROR

| | |
|---|---|
| 30 mph, actual | 31.2 |
| 60 mph | 61.0 |
| 90 mph | 91.9 |

### FUEL CONSUMPTION

| | |
|---|---|
| Normal range, mpg | 12-15 |

### PERFORMANCE

| | |
|---|---|
| Top speed (6800), mph | 133 |
| Shifts, @ mph (manual) | |
| 3rd (6800) | 94 |
| 2nd (6800) | 74 |
| 1st (6800) | 56 |
| Total drag at 60 mph, lb | 115 |

### ACCELERATION

| | |
|---|---|
| 0-30 mph, sec | 2.3 |
| 0-40 | 3.1 |
| 0-50 | 4.3 |
| 0-60 | 5.7 |
| 0-70 | 7.4 |
| 0-80 | 9.3 |
| 0-100 | 14.2 |
| Standing ¼ mile, sec | 14.0 |
| speed at end, mph | 98 |

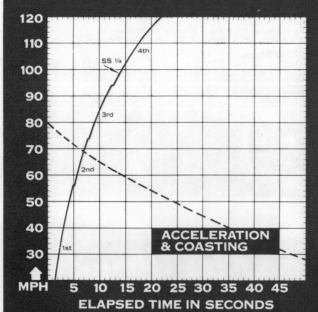

ACCELERATION & COASTING

GRADABILITY IN GEARS

# CORVETTE vs. COBRA

PAUL E. HANSEN PHOTOS

## Pointing Up the Differences, and Similarities, Between Two Fine Road Cars

EVER SINCE THE prototype AC Cobra appeared on the West Coast with entrepreneur Carroll Shelby grinning behind its steering wheel, the verbal battle has been waged. Shortly after Ol' Shel's public introduction of the car, variously comprised teams of competition Cobras appeared on the country's road racing circuits and another sort of battle was begun. The Cobra's arch-rival, of course, was the Chevrolet Corvette, until then the king of the domestic sports car heap.

Although the Cobra, in racing trim at least, has proved the swifter of the two on the road circuit and drag strip, the heated discussions persist between protagonists of each make, who are not willing to concede to the other a single point on which is the best "street" sports car. So, in an attempt to at least organize the discussion, *Car Life* is presenting a point-by-point comparison of the two cars, based on the road test of each.

First, a qualification: We selected the Corvette's most powerful engine (375 bhp, fuel injected) and brake (sintered linings, finned drums) options to give the Sting Ray an even chance. As can be seen by the respective data panels, the test weights figure out to 9.4 lb./bhp for the Cobra, 9.15 lb./bhp for the Corvette. Since the Cobra comes equipped with relatively large disc brakes, it takes the Corvette's full racing option brakes to match the AC's stopping ability. Another equalizing factor: The extra cost of the fuel injection engine, special brakes and knock-off wheels brought the Corvette's retail price to just about equal that of the Cobra.

CHASSIS—Corvette and Cobra share the same basic sort of structure, both depending upon the ladder type of frame layout with sub-structure to support the bodywork. In the case of the Sting Ray coupe, the sub-structure decidedly strengthens the torsional resistance of the chassis. The Cobra's twin-tube design dates back at least 12 years, but if not modern is at least lighter in weight. The Corvette frame, welded up of channel section rails, is overly bulky and heavy for competitive use although it provides a solid, firm platform from which the suspension works.

SUSPENSION—Here is one of the biggest differences between the two cars. They both have fully independent action at all four wheels but the Corvette is by far the more sophisticated in design. Where the front and rear wheel geometry of the Cobra tends to top wheels outward when the car leans during cornering, that of the Corvette tips them inward to keep the tires at a more perpendicular attitude. This, of course, improves the tires' ability to resist skidding, so, at least in theory, the Corvette can corner better than the Cobra. In practice, however, the Cobra has such stiff springs that the car leans hardly at all and cornering traction doesn't suffer too much.

Tires also enter into this picture. The Cobra has Goodyear G-8s as standard equipment, the Corvette Firestone De-Luxe Champions. The G-8s are an ultra-low profile, low cord angle tire developed from Goodyear's stock and sports car racing tires and give fantastic traction. By comparison, the Firestones seem just a bit wobbly and far less capable of resisting side-thrust. Whatever faults the Cobra has in its suspension design, the tires make up for in superior action.

BRAKES—The Cobra has 12 in. discs, the Corvette has 11.5 in. drums. Surprisingly, the Corvette's racing option brakes stopped just as well as, if not better, than did the Cobra's caliper discs. Also surprising, repeated stops from 100 mph produced fading in the Cobra's brakes (and some tail-twitching lock-up of the rear wheels), while the Corvette's brakes withstood the worst we could do without one whit of fade. The data panels show that although the Cobra would out-accelerate the Corvette to 100 mph by 0.8 sec., yet the heftier Corvette could decelerate from 100 mph in 3.1 sec. less time. The 0-100-0 test times for the two were: Cobra, 22.9 sec.; Corvette, 20.6 sec.

BODYWORK—The Cobra's body is of roller-formed aluminum panels, welded into larger panels and hand-finished into a light, smooth unit. The Corvette's body is built up of chopped glass fibers bonded by a polyester resin and formed in

# CORVETTE vs. COBRA

male/female molds to maintain panel gauge and carbon-copy duplication. This fiberglass body is also light, but requires a stronger supporting structure, which adds weight. Although the fiberglass is weather and salt resistant, it is hard to finish smoothly and most Corvettes have a characteristic minute ripple on their finished surfaces.

INTERIORS—Traditional sports car interior design speaks out in the Cobra, where the instruments are simple round-faced dials set into a flat, leather-covered dash panel. All are easy to read at a glance (a big advantage when going fast) and are conveniently located in front of, and to the right of the driver. Ditto the Corvette, although there's a bit more "style" to the whole layout (which adds about 90 lb. extra weight, we're told). Seats on both cars are comfortable in that they fit the driver well enough to give him lateral as well as longitudinal support. The Corvette's seats seemed more softly sprung, and in the long run may be just a bit more comfortable.

DRIVE TRAIN—Both Cobra and Corvette have lightweight, durable, short-stroke V-8s for power and in both cars these engines develop considerably more horsepower than their passenger-sedan brethren. The Corvette, at 1.15 bhp per cu. in is perhaps the more finely tuned (the Cobra has 0.94 bhp/cu. in.), but the fuel injection system is far fussier than the single 4-barrel used on the Cobra. A better comparison here might have been the Corvette's 365-bhp 327 which has a single 4-barrel carburetor atop the fuel-injected's heavy duty block.

In both of these particular power-plants the crankshafts, pistons, rods and bearings are of more durable design and manufacture, the cylinder heads are opened up for better breathing, and the timing and carburetion adjusted to high-speed operation. Both have durability beyond ken, having competed and completed such well-known endurance tests as the Sebring 12-hour race.

The Cobra has the Ford-gearset variation of the Warner Gear T-10 transmission, the Corvette the Muncie 2.20:1 low 4-speed. These are virtually identical units although the Chevrolet gearbox is actually a redesign of the T-10 and probably a little tougher. The Corvette's gears, too, were better spaced, with the 1.28:1 third gear providing a particularly versatile about-town and passing gear.

Final gearing on the Cobra was 3.77:1, for the Corvette it was 4.11:1. However, because the Cobra had those ultra-low profile tires and the Corvette more normal size 15-inchers, the actual miles-per-thousand rpm figures came out comparable. The Corvette has a slightly higher piston-travel-per-mile figure, because of its longer stroke.

PERFORMANCE—Because of the similarities in final gearing, it was no surprise to the test crew that the performance figures for the Cobra and the Corvette were not very far apart. And, using realistic red-line figures for the engine, top speeds are almost identical. Both cars might rev past 7000, but to do so is to risk expensive breakage and the gain in acceleration is negligible, as it puts the next gear up too far past the torque peak.

On the road, there is really no clear-cut choice between the cars. It all comes down to how you like your performance: Firm, nimble and noisy (Cobra) or soft, supple and quiet (Corvette). On high-speed handling, the Corvette has a definite edge, being the more sophisticated in suspension design. But, at low speeds, the lighter Cobra can dart in and out of places that leave the bulkier Corvette panting and puffing, so the fun factor favors the Cobra.

In the final argument, then, the Cobra is just more pure fun to drive, although the Corvette accomplishes the same thing with less fuss and more finesse. ∎

# THE ILLUSTRIOUS AC

CONTINUED FROM PAGE 15

All three wheels, not surprisingly, were independently sprung. Modest though the Petite three-wheelers may have been, they were built with AC's traditional workmanship. There was no difficulty in justifying AC's claim that the Petite was "made a little better than it need be." That's the way they build all their vehicles.

In 1956 a step was taken that made the lithe roadster and coupe even more appealing to discerning motorists. An arrangement was made whereby the 125 bhp Bristol engine could be specified for the Ace, while a 105 bhp Bristol unit became optional for the Aceca. The long-standing AC six was then developing 102 bhp, but it didn't produce as much torque as the Bristols.

With the optional six fitted the Ace would cut out the standing quarter mile in 16.0 sec flat and the top speed approached 115 mph.

To meet the improved performance, disc brakes were offered as optional equipment for the front wheels in 1957. Later that year they became a standard installation on all Ace and Aceca models, although the very efficient Alfin alloy drum brakes were retained at the rear.

Fitted with the 125 bhp engine, the Aceca is only fractionally slower over the standing quarter mile than the lighter Ace. It is interesting to note, however, that the Aceca has a higher top speed — about 130 mph — due to its better aerodynamics.

Came 1959 and AC plucked yet another card from its sleeve — the four seater Greyhound. This was an entirely new car, intended to appeal to those enthusiasts who gave up sports cars because of their shortage of accommodation. Reasonable seating for four adults was provided by lengthening the two-tube chassis 10 inches to give a 100 inch wheelbase and by mounting the engine further forward than in the two-seaters. The Greyhound's frame is not unlike that of the Ace and Aceca, but the suspension is more modern. It maintains AC's good road-holding characteristics, yet promotes an improved ride. The front wheels are controlled by upper and lower wishbones, while those at the rear have a unique arrangement featuring double U-jointed axles and diagonally disposed trailing arms. Coil springs and telescopic dampers are incorporated at all four corners.

Weighing close on a ton, this handsome and desirable four seater has a maximum speed of over 110 mph when fitted with a 128 bhp Bristol engine and overdrive transmission.

As the cars were developed more and more to meet increasing opposition, Rudd realised

that the Bristol engine had shortcomings. It was relatively expensive in the first place and, although very reliable, required constant attention to maintain its peak. Also, there was a definite limit to how much hotting-up could be undertaken without sacrificing durability.

These problems were solved by employing the 2.6-litre, six cylinder Ford engine which normally powers the Zephyr. The Ace 2.6, as it is known, actually costs slightly less than the AC-powered model and undercuts the Bristol by about £350 sterling. The 2.6 is structurally similar to its companions, differing mainly in the frontal styling and transmission.

The bonnet line is two inches lower and the air intake has a more forceful appearance. The Bristol transmission has been replaced by a Moss four speed gearbox of the same type employed by Jaguar.

Ken Rudd has five stages of Ruddspeed conversions to suit the 2.6. The first involves reworking the Ford cylinder head extensively and installing larger valves. With three SU carburettors fitted, the Zephyr pumps out 120 bhp. Adding special pistons and lightweight pushrods (as stage two) gives another five bhp.

The third stage uses a special aluminium alloy cylinder head fitted with two SU carburettors; 140 bhp is then on tap. After fitting custom pistons and another carb, the unit is producing 155 bhp and is still quite suitable for everyday motoring.

The most potent Ruddspeed 2.6 has all the aforementioned goodies, plus a modified camshaft and three Weber carburettors. It develops an honest 170 bhp!

Logically, it is the 155 bhp version that has most appeal for non-racing enthusiasts. And this car, by the way, costs less than the stock 128 bhp Bristol-engined Ace.

The stage four Ruddspeed 2.6 is reported to have immense torque in the mid-rpm range, making it exceptionally tractable. The car's maximum speed of just better than 120 mph may seem out of proportion with the 115 mph maximum of the Ace/Bristol, but it must be appreciated that acceleration is the 2.6s strongest point. The 155 bhp engine's torque enables the Ace to flatten the standing quarter mile in less than 16 seconds. In fact, its time for this distance is only fractionally slower than that required by the E-type Jaguar.

That's the AC story to date. Knowing the pride and care with which AC builds its vehicles (there are currently eight basic versions of the Ace, Aceca and Greyhound), and its realistic approach to good motoring, we feel safe in assuming that there are many more chapters yet to come from this firm.                    #

---

CONTINUED FROM PAGE 43

Connolly of London for AC's experts to cut up and sew into seats over hand-stuffed frames. Pile carpets are hand-cut and hand-seamed, trim panels hand-applied. Door furniture, instruments, minor controls get individual attention from skilled fitters for just as long as it takes to put them right. Even the tubular "sticks" for the soft top are shaped in a corner of the plant and hand-fitted car by car—just as every steering wheel is made up at a little bench in a corner of the machine shop from rings of wood laminate and a stamped alloy frame, every grille put together and installed with loving care by one man with a tray of puzzle-pieces, every giant brake disc

(machined at AC for use with Girling calipers) custom-tested for balance together with its own hub assembly.

All of these processes are in the British automobile manufacturing tradition. The craftsmen who carry them out remember, almost to a man, the days when every car was different and mass-production in any form was a very dirty word. Beside a dusty stockpile of U.S. Ford engines in a dark corner of AC's Thames Ditton factory stands a heap of seasoned, honey-mellow ash framing timber perhaps a quarter-century old. Why does it stand there? "It reminds us," says silver-haired oxy-welder operator, "of a time none of us want to forget."

"Besides, you never know when stuff like that might come in handy . . ."

# GROWING SPEED

If there is anything more competitive than the automobile production business it is the auto racing business. To succeed almost instantly in both fields as Carroll Shelby has done with his Cobra is unprecedented. In only its third year of production, the Cobra has decisively proved itself to be America's best performing sports car. In fact, its reputation is international. Cobra is currently leading competition for the 1965 World Manufacturers Championship. Its acceptance has been so great that founding father Shelby has moved in three short years from a small garage-type location in Santa Fe Springs, Calif., to a 12½-acre facility on the south side of Los Angeles International Airport.

Upon his retirement from competition driving in 1960, Shelby turned his attention to his dream of building a sports car incorporating the raw power which Americans had come to prefer. He found that a new V-8 engine was being developed by Ford Motor Company and after extensive negotiation arranged to mate it with a chassis and aluminum body made in England by A.C. Cars. The first A.C. bodies were delivered to Santa Fe Springs for production in March, 1962. Soon afterwards, Shelby moved the operation to Venice, Calif., where the 260-inch Ford Fairlane originally intended for the Cobra gave way to the 289-inch version. Now a new Cobra, the 427, is in production, incorporating a 427-inch Ford engine, coil spring suspension and a slightly wider and longer body.

Current manufacturing in the 96,000-square foot plant at the 12½-acre airport facility includes 150 Shelby Mustang GT 350's and 50 Cobras per month, in addition to a wide line of Cobra Hi-Performance accessory equipment. Also, the company's Show Car Department handles preparation of Ford's prototype new model automobiles and trucks for Ford publicity and promotion programs.

Shelby American's marketing operation includes the franchising of its own nation-wide system of Shelby American Hi-Performance dealers. The world-famous Shelby American Competition department prepares Cobras and Shelby Mustangs for international and domestic road racing and currently is handling the racing and development of the Ford GT prototype for Ford Motor Company.

# LEGEND

Father of the Cobra, Carroll Shelby, is a mighty proud Texan. His Cobra (hot and cold versions shown at left, above) has put him at the top of the sports car racing fraternity and his GT 350 version of the Mustang (left) has put new teeth into the Ford racing program.

**A few years ago Carroll Shelby had an idea. It took root and sprouted into a new automotive empire.**

Aerial view of new Shelby American plant. Building in foreground contains main production line for street GT 350 Mustangs and street Cobras. Building in back contains show and competition car preparation shop. The racing stable is quartered here.

Raw material for the Cobra mill. In foreground are normal Mustangs as Shelby receives them from Ford. In rear are aluminum Cobra bodies, chassis from AC of England.

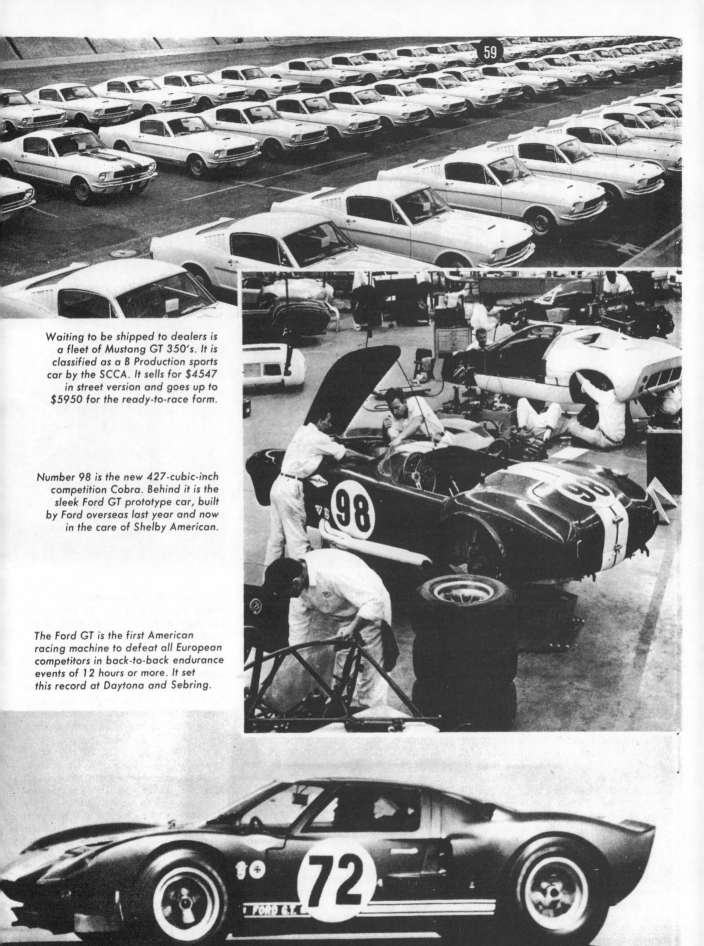

Waiting to be shipped to dealers is a fleet of Mustang GT 350's. It is classified as a B Production sports car by the SCCA. It sells for $4547 in street version and goes up to $5950 for the ready-to-race form.

Number 98 is the new 427-cubic-inch competition Cobra. Behind it is the sleek Ford GT prototype car, built by Ford overseas last year and now in the care of Shelby American.

The Ford GT is the first American racing machine to defeat all European competitors in back-to-back endurance events of 12 hours or more. It set this record at Daytona and Sebring.

# LOTS OF CARS HAVE POWER, BUT FEW HAVE SO MUCH FLEXIBLE POWER AS THE COBRA 427

ROAD TEST

**P**ERIODICALLY, some psychiatrist grabs himself a headline by announcing that the reason men like sports cars is that the car compensates for a sense of sexual inadequacy. We've never bought that theory but if there is anything to it, the cure is simple. ℞: one 427 Cobra.

The most masculine thing about the car is, of course, the power and the deep, throaty rumble that goes with it. The minute it comes to life you know it can do things that no other car can. Lots of cars have power; few have so much flexible power as the Cobra. We accidentally started in 3rd gear instead of 1st once. Except for a momentary lag, it just took off. At the next signal we tried it in 4th with a similar result.

Putting this 425-hp car in motion is less tricky than one might expect. The 11½-inch-diameter single disc clutch is as smooth as any we've ever used, and smooth, easy starts were a cinch. It is just as easy to make a sedate start that won't ruffle your Aunt Harriet as a rubber-burning retina-detaching take-off like a working man's Don Garlits.

Stopping is equally uncomplicated. You step on the brake pedal and the car stops. Period. The Girling disc brakes have neither the bust-your-foot feel often associated with discs nor the sudden lock-up of power brakes. Pedal pressures are relatively high, but not so high as to be tiring.

The car has excellent traffic manners. In the worst summer bumper-to-bumper nightmare, the water temperature remained at 167°F, thanks to an electric fan in front of the radiator. Cockpit temperature in these circumstances became a bit uncomfortable but not unbearable, as in the case of many other high-performance cars. The engine flexibility, already mentioned, takes some of the strain out of traffic too. One can use almost any gear. You aren't likely to over-rev in first, nor lug in 4th, except from a dead standstill. It's not always fun, but we never found it tedious.

When traffic thins out, the Cobra comes into its own as a GT car. The ride, which seems just a bit *too* firm over concrete expansion joints and rough asphalt at 35 or 40 mph, feels just right at 65 or 70 (or more, if you want to tempt fate and lawmen).

Handling, both on the trip to Riverside and in runs at our race course testing site there, was flawless. Considering that the chassis was originally intended for a 2-liter engine, the design modifications for this 7-liter bear are admirable. The old upper transverse leaf spring and lower A-arm system used front and rear in the AC-Bristol and 289 Cobra versions has given way to an all-coil-spring suspension. In all tests on the circuit it went through turns steady and nearly dead flat. If the driver chose a poor line, it was easy to correct with the steering wheel and/or throttle. Entering a turn with too little power would push the front end, but this could be corrected by getting back on the throttle. On very hard right turns, however, the 4-barrel carburetor starved out, which left us with an embarrassing lack of power to get out of the turn. The 8.50 x 15 Goodyear Blue

427-cu.-in. Ford gives the Cobra much more urge (above) than the earlier 289 version, but much redesigning of the suspension enables it to handle the 425 hp as it corners nearly flat (left) at Riverside International Raceway. Unlike the earlier chassis, the 427 never fought back in the corners. Below, the heart of the Cobra, with single Holley 4-barrel carb, chrome-plated Cobra valve covers. Full-competition versions have quartet of 2-barrel Webers, wider wheels and tires, plus special suspension package.

PHOTOS BY FRED ENKE

Dots on 7½-inch magnesium rims gave a very reassuring bite but the fenders flare out far enough to accommodate bigger rubber for serious competition.

With no way to hook our 5th wheel to the tubular bumper, tests were made using the car's own speedometer which had been calibrated. The straightaway at Riverside is inadequate for getting a top-speed figure on such a car, but the ¼-mile and acceleration figures should give a fair idea of just how hairy this beast is.

The cockpit has enough room for tall drivers including space beside the clutch pedal to stretch the left leg on long trips. We were surprised at how easily we adapted to the severely offset pedals. Although we were aware of them at once visually, we had no sensation of being twisted to the left when we got behind the wheel.

The steering wheel is a solid, wood-rimmed affair made for man-sized hands, although it doesn't require comparable strength to turn it. The gearshift lever is capped by a hefty ball, but, unfortu-

Cobra easily smoked tires on acceleration, but new car was too stiff to show its best performance. Note the wide flared fenders.

Magnesium wheels with 3-prong knock-offs are standard equipment, replace the wire wheels used on the early 289 Cobras.

Don't plan to bring much more than a toothbrush and change of socks on trips-- spare tire occupies most of trunk space.

Bucket seats are comfortable, give good support. Instrumentation is complete, but steering wheel hides the tachometer.

# COBRA 427

*continued*

nately, doesn't fall easily to hand. The lever is cranked forward and to one side, but is still too far back for either a tall driver or a short one (like the five-foot-five writer) who must keep the seat well forward. Nonetheless, when you get used to where the shift lever is, there is no trouble, either mechanical or anatomical, shifting into any of the forward gears. Reverse is another story; the location and angle of the lever makes operating the T-handle reverse lockout a bit of a scene.

The car does have some vices that should be mentioned. The horn shares a control lever with the turn signals, and we engendered several dirty looks before we learned to work the latter without setting off the former. The turn signals sometimes cancel, but often don't, something we've seen before with British electrics. The Smiths electric tachometer is very steady, but a spoke in the steering wheel obscures most of it.

Something we never got used to was the reflection in the plastic sun visor of the tail lights of the car ahead, which gave the sensation that the law had caught up with us for some peccadillo.

Wind buffeting in the cockpit is rather more severe than sporty at speeds above 50 mph, and on the trip to the track for the tests we finally resorted to putting on a helmet for comfort. This problem bothered everyone who tried the car, regardless of height. We tried driving with a cowboy hat on and finally concluded that Carroll Shelby must have his sewed to his scalp.

Although amazingly tractable and untemperamental for such a powerful machine, this is clearly not a car for everyone. Assuming you have the money, if you want a car that will cruise effortlessly at high speed and will always give you the feeling that *you* are driving *it*, you can't do better. If you want to pretend that every stop light is the grid at Nurburgring or every freeway the Mulsanne straight, forget it. You can't afford the tickets.
— *Bob Schilling*

## how the car performed . . .

**ACCELERATION (2 aboard)**
0-30 mph. . . . . . . . . . . . . . . . . .1.9 secs.
0-50 mph. . . . . . . . . . . . . . . . . .4.5 secs.
0-60 mph. . . . . . . . . . . . . . . . . .5.3 secs.
0-75 mph. . . . . . . . . . . . . . . . . .8.4 secs.

**TIME & DISTANCE TO ATTAIN PASSING SPEEDS**
40-60 mph. . . . . . . . . . . .2.6 secs., 190.3 ft.
50-70 mph. . . . . . . . . . . .3.5 secs., 308.0 ft.

**STANDING-START ¼-MILE:** 13.8 secs., 106 mph

**BEST SPEEDS IN GEARS @ SHIFT POINTS**
1st . . . . . . . . . . . . . . . . 66 mph @ 6000 rpm
2nd . . . . . . . . . . . . . . . 84 mph @ 6000 rpm
3rd . . . . . . . . . . . . . . . .108 mph @ 6000 rpm
4th . . . . . (not maximum) 110 mph @ 5000 rpm

**MPH PER 1000 RPM: 21**

**STOPPING DISTANCES:** From 30 mph, 31 ft.; from 60 mph, 126 ft.

**SPEEDOMETER ACCURACY**

| Car speedometer | 30 | 45 | 60 | 75 |
|---|---|---|---|---|
| Calibrated speedometer | 30 | 43 | 57 | 70 |

## specifications . . .

**ENGINE IN TEST CAR:** Bore and stroke 4.24 x 3.788 ins. Displacement 427 cu. ins. Advertised hp 425 @ 6500 rpm. Maximum torque 480 lbs.-ft. @ 3500 rpm. Compression ratio 10.4:1. Carburetion 1 4-bbl. Holley.

**TRANSMISSION TYPE & FINAL DRIVE RATIO:** Ford 4-speed. 3.54:1 with limited slip differential.

**SUSPENSION:** All independent with coil springs and unequal length wishbones.

**STEERING:** Rack and pinion. Turning diameter 36 ft., curb to curb. Turns lock to lock 2.5.

**WHEELS:** 7½ x 15 cast alloy.

**TIRES:** 8.50 x 15 Goodyear Blue Dot.

**BRAKES:** Girling disc. Diameter—front 11⅝ ins.; rear, 10¾ ins. Swept disc area, 580 sq. ins.

**SERVICE:** Type of fuel recommended—premium. Fuel capacity 18 gals.

**BODY & FRAME:** Ladder-style tubular frame.

**DIMENSIONS & WEIGHTS:** Wheelbase 90 ins. Track, front and rear 56 ins. Overall length 156 ins., overall width 68 ins., height 49 ins. Minimum ground clearance 4.35 ins. Curb weight 2529 lbs.

**MANUFACTURER'S SUGGESTED LIST PRICE:** $7495— street version (incl. taxes and safety equip't)

**WARRANTY:** 4000 miles and/or 3 months (on street versions only, not competition models)

# SHELBY COBRA 427

## Super cars, beware... there ain't nothin' gonna blow this off the road.

There are fast cars and there are *fast* cars. First to mind in the latter category has to be the Shelby American Cobra 427. It is a big mean looking car that will dust off just about anything on the road without even trying. And that's on any type of road! The only other American-made car that even comes close is the Corvette Sting Ray with the 427 cu. in. engine—and it just comes close.

Forerunner of the present Cobra was the 289 cu. in. version in the old AC body. It had plenty of power and performance, but it was uncomfortable, subject to overheating at just about any legal speed, and had its (ahem!) handling peculiarities. It took a real expert to handle the car, but there were enough of them around to establish Shelby American in the production car business. The 427 is still a brute and should only be driven by above-average

drivers, but even with the extra horsepower it is a much more manageable car.

Contributing a major share towards the Cobra's more agreeable personality is an entirely new suspension. Whereas the old Cobra chassis had about as much torsional rigidity as overcooked spaghetti, the new frame, still fabricated at AC Cars in England—but now to Shelby specifications—is as stiff as a Redwood trunk and permits the equally new coil sprung suspension to operate at maximum efficiency. The man responsible for this all-independent suspension system is Klaus Arning, the Ford Motor Company genius responsible for the impeccable handling of the Ford GT. Arning has designed the same anti-dive and anti-squat characteristics into the 427 Cobra. Under heavy acceleration the car tracks nicely for a machine with such power, and its braking manners are magnificent. The massive Girling discs haul the car down from 100 mph-plus speeds like you've suddenly run into a sand bank, and much of this is due to the suspension's anti-dive capability. Even though things are greatly improved, don't get the impression that this handles like a land cruiser. The car will break traction at speeds beyond 100 mph and imprudent applications of power will send the tail-end slewing sideways. Wider-base

racing tires will help, but the fact remains that the Cobra 427 is not an automobile for novices.

The 427 designation is a misnomer, as the actual engine displacement is 428 cu. in. This all happened midway through the 1966 season when Shelby decided the 427 racing wedge engine was unnecessarily expensive. Ford's 428 cu. in. engine, (also used in the 7 Litre Galaxie sedan), is based on the 352-390 series block and is much less expensive to build than the 427. Ergo, goodbye 427. Performance figures indicate that except for racing applications, there is no real difference in the capabilities of the two engines.

One might expect a Cobra with an engine displacing 428 cu. in. to be an absolute beast on the street. It is utterly to the contrary, with a positively placid disposition at low speeds. This faked us out completely because we expected to find a machine with a vicious, bear-trap clutch and an engine that idled something like a Double-A fuel dragster. We found the 11.5-inch Ford clutch to be no more challenging than a normal domestic unit and the engine ticked off a 700-rpm idle in fine style. In fact, the smoothness of the Cobra at low speeds completely belies its breathtaking performance, and only when the throttle is cracked does one realize the reservoir of power is practically a bottomless pit. Like the engine, the transmission is a standard Ford unit that operates smoothly and efficiently at all speeds and in all gears.

Unlike the 427 Sting Ray, the Cobra has retained its identity as a rawboned, wind-in-the-face sports car. While the Sting Ray is a completely civilized vehicle, available with everything from FM radio to air conditioning, the Cobra comes across the counter with the same spartan aspect that typified pre-Fifties English sports cars. There are side curtains, a top that requires a degree in structural engineering to understand, and, with the top up and the side curtains in place, you're going to find yourself gasping for breath. But if you want air conditioning and all those other creature comforts that are available with a Corvette, you probably aren't interested in a Cobra anyway.

Amazingly, the Cobra engine refused to overheat even in rush-hour traffic. While this worry is gone you're still liable to end up sweating. The men at Shelby have stuffed loads of insulation between the engine and you, but with the engine just a couple of inches from your feet, it still tends to get awfully hot inside the cockpit.

Being about seven inches wider than the old 289, the 427 is a much more comfortable car. The seats are deep, comfortable leather-covered buckets that will accommodate just about any body configuration. The steering wheel is perfectly positioned, though the shift lever comes out of the tunnel about three inches too far aft to be described as ideal and tall drivers will find that they have to twist and bend more than they will like. Gauges and instruments are nicely clustered so that the driver is able to find the information he needs with just a minimum of neck craning.

The 427 Cobra is bulkier looking than its forerunner and, if anything, looks even meaner. It utilizes the same deeply flaired wheel wells that first appeared on the 289 racing versions and, in our highly subjective opinion, is just about the toughest looking car on the road.

The 427 Cobra is sure to be the fastest car on the block, possibly in the state, and if you are of a mind to latch onto one of these twisters Shelby will be glad to take your dough. The 427 Cobra is now available in reasonable quantities and, although your local Ford dealer isn't likely to have two or three in stock, he'll be able to get one into your hot little hands so quickly you won't be able to change your mind.

---

## SHELBY COBRA 427

Manufacturer: Shelby American Inc.
6501 W. Imperial Highway
Los Angeles, Calif.

Price as Tested: $6900

### ENGINE

Water-cooled V-8, cast iron block, 5 main bearings
Bore x stroke .......4.13x3.98 in, 104x101 mm
Displacement.............428 cu. in, 7016 cc
Compression ratio.................10.0 to one
Carburetion ..................1x4-bbl Ford
Valve gear...Pushrod-operated overhead valves, hydraulic lifters
Power (SAE)...........390 bhp @ 5200 rpm
Torque...........475 lbs-ft @ 3700 rpm
Specific power output.....0.91 bhp per cu. in, 55.6 bhp per liter
Mileage...........9-12 mpg on premium fuel
Range on 18-gallon tank .......162-216 miles

### DRIVE TRAIN

Clutch ...........11.5-inch single dry plate
Transmission...........4-speed manual, all-synchromesh

| Gear | Ratio | Overall | Mph/1000 rpm | Max mph |
|------|-------|---------|--------------|---------|
| Rev | 2.32 | 7.68 | −10.86 | −69 |
| 1st | 2.32 | 7.68 | 10.86 | 69 |
| 2nd | 1.69 | 5.59 | 14.98 | 95 |
| 3rd | 1.29 | 4.26 | 19.62 | 124 |
| 4th | 1.00 | 3.31 | 25.12 | 160 |

Final drive ratio.................3.31 to one

### CHASSIS

Wheelbase .........................90 in
Track ...................F: 56  R: 56 in
Length ...........................156 in
Width .............................68 in
Height ............................49 in
Curb Weight ....................2529 lbs
Test Weight ....................2890 lbs
Weight distribution front/rear.......48/52%

Suspension F: Ind., unequal-length wishbones with anti-dive and anti-squat coil springs
R: Ind., unequal-length wishbones with anti-dive and anti-squat coil springs
Brakes........11.6-in discs F, 10.7-in discs R, 580 sq in swept area
Steering...................Rack and pinion
Turns.....................lock to lock 2.5
Turning circle .......................36 ft.
Tires and wheels......8.15x15 on 7.5-in rims

### ACCELERATION

| Zero To | | Seconds |
|---------|-----|---------|
| 30 mph | .................................. | 3.2 |
| 40 " | .................................. | 3.6 |
| 50 " | .................................. | 3.9 |
| 60 " | .................................. | 4.3 |
| 70 " | .................................. | 5.5 |
| 80 " | .................................. | 6.2 |
| 90 " | .................................. | 7.3 |
| 100 " | .................................. | 8.8 |

Standing ¼-mile...........118 mph in 12.2

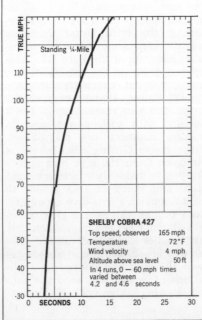

Standing ¼-Mile

**SHELBY COBRA 427**

Top speed, observed    165 mph
Temperature            72°F
Wind velocity          4 mph
Altitude above sea level  50ft
In 4 runs, 0 — 60 mph times varied between 4.2 and 4.6 seconds

---

## CHECK LIST

### ENGINE

Starting .............................Good
Response ..........................Excellent
Noise ...............................Good
Vibration ...........................Good

### DRIVE TRAIN

Clutch Action ......................Excellent
Transmission Linkage ..............Excellent
Syncromesh Action .................Excellent
Power-To-Ground Transmission ........Good

### BRAKES

Response ..........................Excellent
Pedal Pressure .....................Good
Fade Resistance ...................Excellent
Smoothness ........................Excellent
Directional Stability ..............Excellent

### STEERING

Response ............................Good
Accuracy ............................Good
Feedback ............................Good
Road Feel ...........................Good

### SUSPENSION

Harshness Control ...................Good
Roll Stiffness .....................Excellent
Tracking ............................Fair
Pitch Control .......................Good
Shock Damping .....................Excellent

### CONTROLS

Location ............................Good
Relationship ........................Good
Small Controls ......................Good

### INTERIOR

Visibility .........................Excellent
Instrumentation .....................Good
Lighting ............................Good
Entry/Exit ..........................Good
Front Seating Comfort ...............Good
Front Seating Room ..................Good
Rear Seating Comfort ................——
Rear Seating Room ..................——
Storage Space .......................Fair
Wind Noise ..........................Fair
Road Noise ..........................Fair

### WEATHER PROTECTION

Heater ..............................Good
Defroster ...........................Good
Ventilation .........................Poor
Weather Sealing .....................Good
Windshield Wiper Action .............Good

### QUALITY CONTROL

Materials, Exterior .................Good
Materials, Interior .................Good
Exterior Finish .....................Good
Interior Finish .....................Good
Hardware and Trim ...................Good

### GENERAL

Service Accessibility .............Excellent
Luggage Space .......................Poor
Bumper Protection ...................Poor
Exterior Lighting ...................Good
Resistance to Crosswinds ............Good

SCOTT MALCOLM PHOTOS

## *Carroll Shelby's Personal Cobra is the*
# COBRA TO END ALL COBRAS

W E CALLED the 1968 Corvette psychedelic. But that was before we saw Carroll Shelby's new and personal Cobra. All the other mad cars that have passed through the portals of R&T—the Fiberfab Avenger, the Reliant Regal, the Excalibur SS, the Fiat-Abarth OT 1600, the Cyclops, Shelby's own Mustangs and Cobras of past years—all of them pale by comparison. Shel's Cobra is not only the Cobra to end all Cobras—it's the last of the series—but it's the Cobra for the man who has everything. And who's to pretend that Shel doesn't have everything?

So what's different about Carroll Shelby's Cobra? First, last, and most, two—count 'em, two—whopping Paxton superchargers atop the already potent (about 450 bhp) 427 engine. Each of them feeding a huge Holley 4V carburetor. Each of them delivering 6 psi pressure to the carburetor. How much power? Shelby says 800 bhp. That might be stretching it a bit. Perhaps one should just fall back on the old Rolls-Royce answer and say, "adequate."

Behind this incredible engine, everything is pretty normal; just a few little touches to complete the picture properly. A beefy Ford T6 3-speed automatic transmission drives through a 3.31:1 limited-slip differential and the standard Cobra independent rear suspension to 12.10-15 Goodyear tires on 9.5-in. wheels. With no clutch to deliver shock loads to the rear wheels, the big tires have no trouble at all putting the tremendous torque to the ground.

In the cockpit is a marvelous array of instruments, enough of them to warm the heart of any pureblooded enthusiast. In front of the driver are the essentials demanded by any race driver: tachometer, oil pressure and water temperature gauges. The tach reads to 8000 rpm. Out in the center array are a 180-mph speedometer, ammeter, fuel pressure and oil pressure gauges, blower pressure gauges, and intake manifold vacuum gauges that read also into the positive side of the scale when the blowers are going full tilt. Blower pressure

and manifold pressure readings are nearly identical under full pressure conditions. Two auxiliary electric fuel pumps supplement the engine's mechanical pump when the extra supply is needed. And believe us, it'll be needed if the performance potential is used, for the gentlest driving nets just about 9 mpg!

Not wishing to hide his candle under a bushel, Shel had his metalbenders dress up the Cobra a bit here and there. A giant hood bubble clears the two blowers and forms a big airscoop at the front. The exhaust headers emerge chromed from the front fender and blend into a large collector/small muffler on each side before giving their all to unsuspecting bystanders just ahead of the rear wheels. Our photographer Scott Malcolm still has a raw red calf from *that*. A chrome rollbar and competition seat belts furnish crash protection. The delicate aluminum bodywork has been bent, smoothed and painted beautifully (a dark metallic blue) by Shelby's body shop, but the finish won't last long if the rear tires keep scraping their fenders and hapless road testers continue to get caught on roads with bits of gravel strewn about. Those latter particles all leave small outward dings in the aluminum surface, as there are no inner fender panels. The car weighs 2500 lb, full of lubricants and water and with 10 gallons fuel.

With a double-blown 7-liter and three fuel pumps to make demands upon it, the fuel tank is adequate for some traveling at 42 gallons. That's the regular competition Cobra capacity.

By this time the reader just might be wondering what it's like to drive a machine like this. Well, there's one thing above all: it's *conspicuous*. Besides simply looking like the meanest thing short of a Group 7, it also sounds that way. The engine does idle at about 700 with the transmission engaged but not without audible protest. And holding the car against the torque converter goes from *tough* with the engine idling to *well-nigh impossible* with it revved up. This latter condition forced us to make simple, drive-off starts in our ac-

*Monstrous hood bubble clears blowers and gathers fresh air.*
*Notice the ultra-smooth bodywork and beautiful paintwork.*

*Ford T-bar selects ranges for the automatic transmission.*
*All four small instruments on right deal with superchargers.*

# END-ALL COBRA

celeration tests. Not only did the engine tend to load up when we attempted to get it up to converter stall speed, but we physically couldn't hold the car still with the brakes! The brakes are vacuum assisted, but—wow!

Anyhow, Shel's Cobra may not be exactly designed for ambling about town, but that's what it winds up doing most of the time and it does it well, everything considered. The alternator-water pump belt came off while we had the car, but prior to that it showed no tendency to overheat in traffic. The engine makes a lot of fuss at idle, but it's always ready to move flexibly off from the traffic lights.

But the fun comes when you can put your *FOOT IN IT*. And when you do, prepare to be impressed and compressed!

We took it to our favorite dragstrip, Orange County Raceway, for the acceleration tests. With OCR's electronic timing in action we got readings of 11.86 sec for the standing ¼-mi with a final speed of 115.5 mph. We let the automatic shift for itself at 6200 rpm, as there was nothing to be gained by taping it on to the allowable 7000 rpm. Now, that may not sound startling. But, mind you, that was achieved *without wheelspin*! The blue Cobra doesn't get off the line like a cannon shot, but when those blowers start whining . . .

Top speed? We didn't run it. The Cobra isn't an aerodynamic wonder, but 182 @ 7000 rpm seems reasonable with the output and the gearing. By the way, a duplicate of the car has been built for entertainer Bill Cosby. So you're twice as likely to see one of these monsters roaming about. Beware.

As mentioned last month, the "classic" Cobra is now out of production in the U.S. The Shelby and Cosby cars are the final two examples to be built so this machine is, literally, the Cobra to end all Cobras.

*It's madness . . . sanitary installation of two Paxton blowers tops off a chrome-bedecked 427 engine for adequate power.*

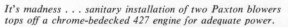

## ACCELERATION

Time to distance, sec:

| | |
|---|---|
| 0–100 ft | 2.6 |
| 0–250 ft | 4.5 |
| 0–500 ft | 7.0 |
| 0–750 ft | 9.0 |
| 0–1000 ft | 10.6 |
| 0–1320 ft (¼ mi) | 11.9 |
| Speed at end, mph | 116 |

Time to speed, sec:

| | |
|---|---|
| 0–30 mph | 2.2 |
| 0–40 mph | 2.6 |
| 0–60 mph | 3.8 |
| 0–80 mph | 5.6 |
| 0–100 mph | 7.9 |
| 0–120 mph | 13.6 |
| 0–140 mph | 24.4 |
| Passing exposure time, sec: | |
| To pass car going 50 | 2.1 |

## SPEEDS IN GEARS

| | | |
|---|---|---|
| 3rd gear (7000 rpm), mph | | 182 |
| 2nd | (7000) | 126 |
| 1st | (7000) | 75 |

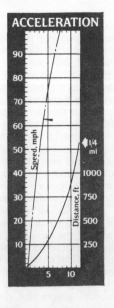

ACCELERATION

**Sam Posey and the C/D staff**
**Compare Detroit's 1970 Performance Cars**

# SS454 CHEVELLE·DUSTER 340
# MUSTANG BOSS 302

**To The Ultimate of the '60s**

# SHELBY AC COBRA

PHOTOGRAPHY: HUMPHREY SUTTON

**T**hrough the windshield the horizon is tilted. Neck muscles strain against G-forces to support the weight of a crash helmet. Senses are bombarded with sounds —the painful scream of tires against asphalt, the belligerent roar of a 289 Ford— and smells; good British leather and traces of gasoline vapor. We are halfway through the Hook. Lime Rock's unforgiving hairpin that is conquered with two carefully chosen apexes or not at all. The black Cobra snorts and bellows against an unseen force as Sam Posey works on the huge wooden steering wheel, correcting minute slides before they become malignant. He shouts over the auditory assault, "No doubt about it, this has the feel of a real racing car— very, very serious."

His description couldn't have been more accurate. The Shelby Cobra was as menacing as its name from the very first. With malice aforethought it attacked and annihilated the Corvettes in SCCA's A/production, and after that taste of blood a coupe-bodied version went on to win its class at Le Mans in 1964. So successful was it as a racer that it was the first car to break Ferrari's hold on the World Manufacturers Championship in the years after that title became based on competition among production automobiles. It is a single purpose car—a powerful, high-winding V-8 in a stark, lightweight English AC chassis— for men who equate truth with speed and agility, and ask for nothing more. Production ceased in 1966 but the Cobra's performance still stands as a high water mark for all to see. It is the yardstick by which all other performance cars must be measured.

Today a yardstick (and a long one at that) is essential if we are to comprehend the improvements Detroit is engineering into its performance cars. The need became obvious this past summer as we previewed the 1970 models. Small cars are being outfitted with big engines—medium-size cars have engines that are enormous. Wheels and tires are now as wide as what you would have found on pure racing cars a few years ago, and truly sophisticated handling packages (many with rear anti-sway bars) are standard equipment. The point was forcefully pounded home at the GM proving grounds when we discovered that a Buick GS455 (of all things), loaded down to 4300 pounds with every conceivable comfort option, would still drive circles around an Opel GT, a "sports car," on the handling course. Detroit is building some very athletic automobiles, not just in acceleration but in handling and braking as well. Urged on by our natural curiosity about the sporting side of these devices we set out to ascertain the state of the art in Detroit.

Thanks to model proliferation, testing every one of Detroit's super cars is out of the question—it would take about five years for the task. Instead, we would take a sample, one car from each of the three distinct performance car categories, and

see how they measured up to the Cobra yardstick. Which cars? Well, there had to be an intermediate sedan because that is what Detroit's super cars have been since the beginning. Chevrolet is fixing to sell a 450-horsepower SS454 Chevelle—the highest advertised horsepower rating in all of Detroit—and that is reason enough that it should be in the test. Walter Mackenzie, a gray-haired veteran of Chevrolet's diplomatic corps, was up for the idea as soon as we phoned him. He remembered the Cobra ("You mean that low, skinny, lightweight thing?") and what it had done to the Corvettes and he wanted just one more chance. Production of the 450-hp Chevelle wasn't scheduled until January—but there were engines and there were cars—it was just a matter of putting the two together. Not to worry—there would be an SS454 Chevelle for the test.

Of course, there had to be a sporty car. These scrappy coupes have hyped up the Trans-Am Series popularity to the point where it threatens to eclipse the Can-Am. Deciding on a representative from this class was more difficult. Eventually, all the big engine versions were dismissed in favor of the 5-liter, Trans-Am-inspired models because they specialize in carefully tailored overall performance rather than merely dazzling acceleration. We finally settled on the Boss 302 Mustang for the most straightforward of all reasons—we just like to drive it. We've been enchanted by its capabilities since we drove the first prototype in Dearborn (*C/D*, June '69) and Brock Yates has proven that a mildly modified Boss can be competitive in SCCA regional racing (*C/D*, January '69) while still remaining streetable. After all of this favorable experience we wanted to see how an absolutely stock Boss ranked on Cobra yardstick.

That left one category to be filled—a category that we feel is the start of a trend. For a long time we've been questioning Detroit's logic in concentrating its performance efforts on the heavy intermediate-size cars when there were lighter

models around which could do the same job but with smaller engines and, ultimately, less expense to the customer. Plymouth's junior Road Runner, the Duster 340, is a giant step in this sensible direction. By including a Duster in the test we could get an early reading on the validity of the concept and perhaps even encourage its growth. But in Detroit our motives were not so transparent. Plymouth felt picked upon. Remembering past *C/D* comparison tests designed to ferret out the most capable car in a given class, Plymouth figured it had been singled out for the booby prize. "What are you guys trying to do? How can a Duster compete against a 454 Chevelle?" The Cobra was obviously beyond comprehension. "Let us bring a Hemi Cuda. That'll show those bastids." But we finally convinced Plymouth that this wasn't the apples-to-pumpkins comparison test that it appeared to be. In fact, it wasn't a comparison test in the conventional sense at all. Rather, it was to be the definitive statement on the whole range of Detroit performance cars, using as reference what most enthusiasts consider to be the world's fastest production car, the Shelby Cobra.

And, of course, we had to have a Cobra. Because it was the 289 that established the Cobra's all conquering reputation we chose that model. The 427 is faster, to be certain, but in reality it only made the Cobra legend burn a bit more brightly. Besides, classifying the big-engined brute as a production car is something of a dubious practice since only about 200 of them were built.

Cobras are where you find them. Walter Perkins, a bright young engineer with a bumper crop of red hot corpuscles, had a well-oiled 1965 model—bright, shiny and unmodified—that he figured was more than a match for any Chevelle, 454 or otherwise. We would find out. So would Sam Posey, our consulting arbitrator, who can be counted upon to hand down a decision in effusive pear-shaped tones. Posey is perfect for the job. That he is an intrepid

*Front lock-up on the Chevelle makes for a straight, if smokey, stop while rear lock-up aims the Mustang at the guard rail.*

competition driver is merely a proven fact, but his ability to drive to the ragged edge in anything with wheels *and* coolly describe its behavior in detail at the same time is a source of wonderment. And no one knows the way around Lime Rock better than he does. Any lingering doubts about that should have been erased by his two professional-series victories there in this past season alone; one in a Shelby-prepared Trans-Am Mustang and the other in his Formula A McLaren-Chevrolet. With this kind of background our 4-car road test couldn't help but be revealing.

A varied group converged at Lime Rock on the appointed day—a handful of escapees from the C/D office; Posey and his stopwatch expert, John Whitman; Bill Howell, an engineering wizard from Chevrolet who can always be found stalking around in the pits at Trans-Ams making sure that Chevrolet isn't racing; Don

Wahrman from Ford, one of Jacque Passino's disciples; and a couple of Detroit-owned PR men whose job is always to influence the outcome if possible. Plymouth had planned to send an engineering-type but the one chosen fell off a motorcycle at the last minute and couldn't make it. Perkins and Mrs. Perkins arrived with the Cobra and everything was set.

The cars had arranged themselves as to straight-line performance the day before at New York National. Perkins had kept the Cobra reputation alive by charging his machine through the quarter at 101.58 mph in 13.73 seconds—a scant 0.08 seconds ahead of the Chevelle—proving that there is no substitute for weight distribution. The Chevelle was decidedly more powerful, pushing its 3885-pound bulk through the traps at 103.80 mph, but with 57.1% of its weight on the front wheels it just couldn't quite get a good enough

grip on the asphalt to move out ahead of the Cobra. The big 454 did prove itself however. It is a fairly straightforward derivative of the 435-hp Corvette 427 with a 0.24-inch longer stroke and a single 780 cubic-feet-per-minute Holley 4-bbl. instead of the Corvette's three 2-bbls. Because its solid-lifter valve train is very stable at high engine speeds, Howell felt that 6500 rpm wasn't an unreasonable redline—even though the Chevelle seemed to go just as quickly when shifted at 6000.

Just behind the Cobra and Chevelle in acceleration was the Duster. At 3368 pounds it was the lightest of the Detroit cars—though still 1046 pounds heavier than the Cobra. It also had the best weight distribution of all the Detroit iron with exactly 55% on the front. Its quarter-mile performance of 14.39 seconds at 97.2 was hampered by a balky shift mechanism but, even so, the Duster speaks well for the compact super car concept.

The Mustang turned out to be a disappointment. It was only a bit heavier than the Duster, 3415 pounds with a full tank, but it was significantly less powerful, something we hadn't expected from an engine that was developed specifically for racing. When our best efforts were no better than 14.93 seconds at 93.45 mph we asked Wahrman to try, just to see if the factory knew something about driving Boss 302s that we didn't. In the best drag racer, gas-pedal-flat-to-the-floor tradition, he made two runs but neither bettered the Mustang's standings. The real point to be made here is that small displacement, high specific output engines suffer mightily in passing the exhaust emission and exhaust noise standards. Now that the SCCA allows production engines to be destroked down to the 5-liter maximum for the Trans-Am, the high performance 302s will soon disappear as a production option. In fact, the Boss 302 is the only one left right now.

That the acceleration portion of the test was out of the way meant that we had the whole day to evaluate handling and breaking at Lime Rock with Posey. Braking distances and cornering speeds would be measured, and to understand the behavior of each car as it approached the limit, one of the staff would ride along on all but the fastest laps to record Posey's observations. In the lead-off spot was the Chevelle.

We could have predicted Posey's first comment, which came within 100 feet after pulling onto the track.

"Oh, look at that little louver. Whenever I accelerate a little trapdoor on the hood opens."

It is a great piece of entertainment. With the "Cowl Induction" option, Chevrolet's version of a hood scoop, a little backwards-facing hatch at the rear of the hood opens whenever manifold vacuum drops below a predetermined value. In goes cold air and up goes horsepower or something like that. But Posey's next observation was far more serious.

"The rear view mirror is placed exactly where I want to look for a right turn. I have to scrunch down if I want to see."

This has been a problem in many Detroit cars since the federal safety standards requiring larger rear view mirrors went into effect. Now you have a blind spot in front instead of behind, which is a most unsatisfactory trade-out. And there were more comments about the interior.

"The driving position is really quite good but I can't brace my knees against the side panel—it is too far away. I just have to hold on to the steering wheel."

The observations continued in a calm, analytic flow, but there was absolutely nothing calm about what he was doing with the Chevelle. Three-digit numbers on the speedometer, airborne over the brow of the hill, 6000 rpm on the tach—the straights were now brief bursts of

## SHELBY AC COBRA

**Price as tested:** $6167.00

**Options on test car:** dress-up group, $172.00 (price does not include chrome wire wheels or hardtop).

### ENGINE
| | |
|---|---|
| Bore x stroke | 4.00 x 2.87 in |
| Displacement | 289 cu in |
| Compression ratio | 10.5 to one |
| Carburetion | 1 x 4-bbl Autolite |
| Power (SAE) | 271 hp @ 6000 rpm |
| Torque (SAE) | 312 lbs-ft @ 3400 rpm |

### DRIVE TRAIN
| | |
|---|---|
| Final drive ratio | 3.77 to one |

### DIMENSIONS AND CAPACITIES
| | |
|---|---|
| Wheelbase | 90.0 in |
| Track | F: 51.5 in, R: 52.5 in |
| Length | 151.5 in |
| Width | 61.0 in |
| Height | 49.0 in |
| Curb weight | 2322 lbs |
| Weight distribution, F/R | 48.5/51.5% |

### SUSPENSION
F: Ind., lower wishbones, upper transverse leaf spring
R: Ind., lower wishbones, upper transverse leaf spring

### STEERING
| | |
|---|---|
| Type | Rack and pinion |
| Turns lock-to-lock | 2.75 |
| Turning circle | 34.0 ft |

### BRAKES
| | |
|---|---|
| F | 11.6-in disc |
| R | 10.8-in disc |

### WHEELS AND TIRES
| | |
|---|---|
| Wheel size | 15 x 6.0-in |
| Tire make and size | Goodyear F70-15, polyester |
| Test inflation pressure | F: 30 psi, R: 30 psi |

### PERFORMANCE
| Zero to | Seconds |
|---|---|
| 40 mph | 2.7 |
| 60 mph | 5.2 |
| 80 mph | 8.5 |
| 100 mph | 13.4 |
| Standing ¼-mile | 13.73 sec @ 101.58 mph |
| 80-0 mph panic stop | 256 ft (0.84 G) |

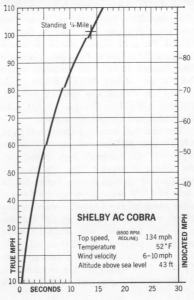

**SHELBY AC COBRA**

| | | |
|---|---|---|
| Top speed, | (6500 RPM REDLINE) | 134 mph |
| Temperature | | 52°F |
| Wind velocity | | 6-10 mph |
| Altitude above sea level | | 43 ft |

## MUSTANG BOSS 302

**Price as tested:** $4318.45

**Options on test car:** fastback coupe with Boss package (includes: 290-hp engine, bucket seats, 4-speed transmission, front disc brakes, racing mirrors, collapsible spare, quick-ratio steering, competition suspension, front spoiler, carpets, gauges, fiberglass belted tires), $3720.00; rear spoiler, $20.00; limited-slip differential, $43.00, 3.91 rear axle, $13.00; convenience check group, $32.00; sport slats, $65.00; AM/FM stereo radio, $214.00; decor group, $78.00; tinted glass, $32.00; deluxe belts, $15.00; HD battery, $13.00; tachometer $54.00.

### ENGINE
| | |
|---|---|
| Bore x stroke | 4.00 x 3.00 in |
| Displacement | 302 cu in |
| Compression ratio | 10.6 to one |
| Carburetion | 1 x 4-bbl Holley |
| Power (SAE) | 290 hp @ 5800 rpm |
| Torque (SAE) | 290 lbs-ft @ 4300 rpm |

### DRIVE TRAIN
| | |
|---|---|
| Final drive ratio | 3.91 to one |

### DIMENSIONS AND CAPACITIES
| | |
|---|---|
| Wheelbase | 108.0 in |
| Track | F: 59.5 in, R: 59.5 in |
| Length | 187.4 in |
| Width | 71.7 in |
| Height | 50.2 in |
| Curb weight | 3415 lbs |
| Weight distribution, F/R | 55.9/44.1% |

### SUSPENSION
F: Ind., unequal-length control arms, coil springs, anti-sway bar
R: Rigid axle, semi-elliptic leaf springs, anti-sway bar

### STEERING
| | |
|---|---|
| Type | Recirculating ball |
| Turns lock-to-lock | 3.6 |
| Turning circle | 38 ft |

### BRAKES
| | |
|---|---|
| F | 11 3 in vented disc, power assist |
| R | 10.0 x 2.0-in cast iron drum, power assist |

### WHEELS AND TIRES
| | |
|---|---|
| Wheel size | 15 x 7.0-in |
| Tire make and size | Goodyear F60-15, Polyglass |
| Test inflation pressure | F: 28 psi, R: 28 psi |

### PERFORMANCE
| Zero to | Seconds |
|---|---|
| 40 mph | 3.3 |
| 60 mph | 6.5 |
| 80 mph | 11.1 |
| 100 mph | 17.0 |
| Standing ¼-mile | 14.93 sec @ 93.45 mph |
| 80-0 mph panic stop | 296 ft (0.72 G) |

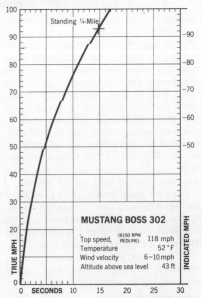

**MUSTANG BOSS 302**

| | | |
|---|---|---|
| Top speed, | (6150 RPM REDLINE) | 118 mph |
| Temperature | | 52°F |
| Wind velocity | | 6-10 mph |
| Altitude above sea level | | 43 ft |

## CHEVELLE SS454

**Price as tested:** $4470.05

**Options on test car:** Chevelle coupe, $2809.00; SS package $445.55; 450-hp engine, $263.30; automatic transmission, $290.40; power steering, $105.35; bucket seats, $121.15; deluxe belts, $12.15; floor mats, $11.60; door edge guards, $4.25; vinyl roof, $94.80; console, $53.75; visor vanity mirror, $3.20; cushioned rim steering wheel, $34.80; AM/FM radio, $133.80; rear speaker, $13.20; bumper guards, $15.80, clock, $15.80; limited-slip differential, $42.15.

### ENGINE
Bore x stroke.....................4.25 x 4.00 in
Displacement......................454 cu in
Compression ratio...............11.0 to one
Carburetion.........1 x 4-bbl Holley, 780 cfm
Power (SAE)...........450 hp @ 5200 rpm
Torque (SAE).........500 lbs-ft @ 3600 rpm

### DRIVE TRAIN
Final drive ratio....................3.70 to one

### DIMENSIONS AND CAPACITIES
Wheelbase.........................112.0 in
Track...............F: 60.0 in, R: 59.8 in
Length............................197.2 in
Width.............................75.4 in
Height............................56.2 in
Curb weight.......................3885 lbs
Weight distribution, F/R..........57.1/42.9%

### SUSPENSION
F: Ind., unequal-length control arms, coil springs, anti-sway bar
R: Rigid axle, trailing arms, coil springs, anti-sway bar

### STEERING
Type...........Recirculating ball, power assist
Turns lock-to-lock.....................2.9
Turning circle.........................42.0 ft

### BRAKES
F:............11.0-in vented disc, power assist
R:....9.5 x 2.2-in cast iron drum, power assist

### WHEELS AND TIRES
Wheel size....................14 x 7.0-in
Tire make and size.........Goodyear F70-14, polyester
Test inflation pressure....F: 35 psi, R: 35 psi

### PERFORMANCE
Zero to                 Seconds
  40 mph...........................2.9
  60 mph...........................5.4
  80 mph...........................8.7
  100 mph..........................13.0
Standing ¼-mile.....13.81 sec @ 103.80 mph
80–0 mph panic stop...........272 ft (0.79 G)

## VALIANT DUSTER 340

**Price as tested:** $3455.70

**Options on test car:** Duster 340, $2547.00; bucket seats, $112.60; light package, $29.60; basic group, $82.60; decor group, $23.90; deluxe seat belts, $13.75; 4-speed transmission, $187.90; limited-slip differential, $42.35; special paint, $14.05; 50-amp alternator, $11.00; 59-amp battery, $12.95; tinted windshield, $20.40; day-night mirror, $7.10; dual horns, $5.15; pedal dress up, $5.45; undercoat, $16.60; door edge molding, $4.65; custom sill, $13.15; wheel lip molding, $7.60; belt molding, $13.60; bumper guards, $23.80; tach, $50.15; power steering, $85.15; vinyl roof, $83.95; vinyl side molding, $14.80; E70 tires, $26.45.

### ENGINE
Bore x stroke.....................4.04 x 3.31 in
Displacement......................340 cu in
Compression ratio...............10.5 to one
Carburetion...............1 x 4-bbl Carter AVS
Power (SAE)...........275 hp @ 5000 rpm
Torque (SAE).........340 lbs-ft @ 3200 rpm

### DRIVE TRAIN
Final drive ratio....................3.91 to one

### DIMENSIONS AND CAPACITIES
Wheelbase.........................108.0 in
Track...............F: 57.7 in, R: 55.6 in
Length............................188.4 in
Width.............................71.6 in
Height............................52.6 in
Curb weight.......................3368 lbs
Weight distribution, F/R..........55.0/45.0%

### SUSPENSION
F: Ind., unequal-length control arms, torsion bars, anti-sway bar
R: Rigid axle, semi-elliptic leaf springs

### STEERING
Type...........Recirculating ball, power assist
Turns lock-to-lock.....................3.6
Turning circle.........................41.0 ft

### BRAKES
F:............10.8-in vented disc, power assist
R:....10.0 x 1.8-in cast iron drum, power assist

### WHEELS AND TIRES
Wheel size....................14 x 5.5-in
Tire make and size.........Goodyear E70-14
Test inflation pressure....F: 35 psi, R: 35psi

### PERFORMANCE
Zero to                 Seconds
  40 mph...........................3.0
  60 mph...........................5.9
  80 mph...........................9.9
  100 mph..........................15.1
Standing ¼-mile.....14.39 sec @ 97.2 mph
80–0 mph panic stop...........287 ft (0.74 G)

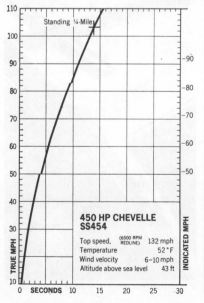

**450 HP CHEVELLE SS454**

| Top speed, (6500 RPM REDLINE) | 132 mph |
| Temperature | 52°F |
| Wind velocity | 6–10 mph |
| Altitude above sea level | 43 ft |

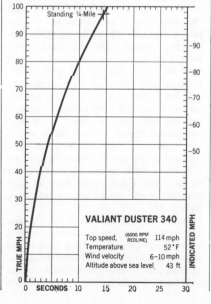

**VALIANT DUSTER 340**

| Top speed, (6000 RPM REDLINE) | 114 mph |
| Temperature | 52°F |
| Wind velocity | 6–10 mph |
| Altitude above sea level | 43 ft |

wide-open throttle and the curves abrupt changes of heading.

"The brakes are good for only about two laps and then they begin to fade. While they're working they are predictable, though. The biggest problem is the abrupt downshifts in the automatic transmission which breaks the tires loose and throws the rear end out. To get good control I have to shift manually at some point where I can stand a little twitch."

When it came to getting around corners the Chevelle proved to be quite agile in Posey's hands.

"The engineers who did this thing understand their problem—all that weight up front—and I think they've coped very well. The track is rough and the bumps are not throwing it off badly. It understeers but the understeer kind of cancels out the bumps. When the front tires are at the limit the rears aren't working so hard, just enough so they get some power to the ground and contend with the bumps too. Now, if we were teetering through these corners in an oversteer posture the car would be very sensitive to them."

From the lap times it was obvious that he was getting along well with the Chevelle. Already he was down to 1:10:4, which is a very good time for a street car. How would the other super car, the Duster, do? It was time to find out.

"For a gearshift here, hell, it looks like a stick for pole vaulting. And the funny little round knob. I don't know why they tried to make it look like wood. It is one of the most conspicuously fake things I've ever set my eyes on. Look at the little tach. It's *tiny*. I do like looking out over the orange hood though—gives me just a hint of being a McLaren driver. I'm a little apprehensive about all of this noise. We are going to have to shout."

After the smooth, quiet Chevelle the Duster was a vivid contrast. It rattled and buzzed at anything approaching speed and just generally broadcasted the same vibrance that made the Model A Ford seem so sophisticated in its day. As he started to work on faster lap times Posey wasn't optimistic.

"The power steering has nowhere near the road feel of the Chevelle and the car is not reacting well to the Gs. The suspension doesn't feel like the final solution. I don't detect the subtle hand of Colin Chapman in the geometry. What's happening is that as the body rolls in the turns it uses up all of the suspension travel and comes right in solid against the rubber bumpers. At that instant the weight transfer is complete on that wheel and the tire takes a terrible beating."

And, all the while the poor confused little Duster is being hurled around the track in a fashion it never dreamed possible. Through the Hook and into the Esses, tail out, tires howling and the lion-hearted 340 moaning spasmodically as Sam played the throttle for just the right amount of torque.

| CORNERING CAPABILITY | | | | |
|---|---|---|---|---|
| | Cobra | Chevelle | Mustang | Duster |
| Average speed through HOOK | 67.5 mph | 66.0 mph | 64.6 mph | 63.9 mph |
| Average speed through ESSES | 63.8 mph | 61.4 mph | 61.1 mph | 60.2 mph |

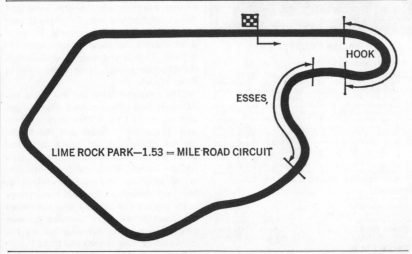

LIME ROCK PARK—1.53 = MILE ROAD CIRCUIT

"It is both understeering and oversteering simultaneously, which is to say that it's sliding right off the road. The carburetor isn't helping either. It cuts out at the most inopportune times. Also, I'm having a lot of trouble with the shift, particularly into third."

The shifter problem is unfortunate. Chrysler buys the Hurst linkage, but because of confusion on the part of the executives as to which is most important, a solid, dependable shift or total absence of noise, the engineers are forced to rubber isolate the shifting mechanism to the point where its usefulness in changing gears is merely coincidental. And the tall lever contributes its share to the confusion by making the throw unreasonably long. Even though the Duster was having its problems Sam wasn't ready to give up.

"Notice that the tires are leaving black marks in the turns which suggests that they need more pressure."

With a best lap of 1:13.95 the Duster didn't appear to be much of a threat to the Cobra. Still, with more air in the tires it figured to improve. As the pressures were being raised from 30 to 35 psi we went on to the Mustang.

"The instruments may be at the end of the Holland Tunnel down there. They are big enough but still difficult to read because of the complex markings. The driving position is a bit peculiar. The steering wheel is plenty close but the floor is too far away to brace my left foot satisfactorily. A telescoping steering column would be a good idea. This car has far more lateral support than the others and it feels very solid and secure."

We had been impressed by the same sensation when driving the Mustang on the road. It is quiet and exudes quality, very much like an expensive European GT car. The stiff suspension and high shock absorber control give it a very purposeful feel, and because the body doesn't quiver or rattle when you hit a bump the overall impression is most satisfying.

"With the manual steering it feels very heavy up front, particularly after the Duster which, although it didn't generate high lateral forces, was very easy to toss around. The steering effort is extremely high—certainly higher than any race car."

Within a few laps the Mustang's virtues and vices, which tend to be extreme, were laid out for inspection.

"The brakes are fabulous. I can go in way deeper before I have to brake with this car than I could with the other cars. And the pedal feel is excellent. Here, I can control the braking with pressure on the pedal where in the other cars the pressure stays about the same and the braking seems to depend on how far down I push the pedal. That is very tricky to do accurately, especially when you are going fast. But boy, does it understeer. Look, you'd think I was going into the pretzel business with my arms. I've got the wheel really cranked over and it just isn't getting the job done. The only way I can get the tail out is to trick it by hitting a bump at just the right time or setting it up with the brakes. Funny, I expect more of this car in handling than it's giving me. And it's busting my hands. Every time we hit a bump in the turns the wheel kicks back so hard that I can hardly hold on to it with my arms crossed up the way they have to be."

With a best lap of 1:12.35 the Mustang had been quicker than the Duster, but only with considerable effort. Once back in the pits the hardships of manual steering and extreme understeer were obvious for all to see. Sam's hands, in the crotch between

the thumb and first finger, were bruised and swollen from being battered by the steering wheel spokes. The front tires hadn't escaped either. The outer tread rib was badly shredded—so bad, in fact, that it looked like the tread might start to peel. This brings up an interesting point about wide tires like the Mustang's F60-15s. Chevrolet is reluctant to use them, particularly on cars like the Chevelle, because the front suspension camber pattern is such that it lifts the inside of the tread patch in hard cornering to the point where the front tires are operating at a disadvantage relative to the rears—which exaggerates understeer. Curiously, the Chevelle wasn't wearing bias-belted tires (which are standard equipment this year) but rather last year's Goodyear bias-ply, polyester cord Wide Tread GTs. As a point of interest, the Cobra and the Chevelle both had exactly the same type of tires.

With the preliminaries out of the way it was time to explore the limits of Detroit performance. The Chevelle was charging around the track, its ears laid back and its hood louver snapped open to battle position. In compliance with California noise laws the exhaust has been restricted to a benevolent rumble, but the air rushing into the carburetor to feed those 454 cubic inches sounded like it was trying to take half the landscape with it. The Chevelle is a big car, enormous on Lime Rock, a tight, twisty, 1.53-mile circuit normally inhabited by Formula Vees and other assorted fruit-cup racers, but it didn't matter. Across the start-finish line at 110 mph, hard on the brakes for the Hook, wheels cocked in for the turn and clipping the infield grass at the apex—it seemed right at home. And it was doing very well, too. With a best lap of 1:08:00 it was the fastest non-race car that Jim Haynes, the track manager, could remember. The cornering speeds were good too—

*The "louver," more fun than functional.*

## COBRA VS. THE 1970'S

*Continued*

66.0 mph through the Hook and 61.4 mph through the Esses, a section with a left/right transition that is difficult for softly sprung passenger cars.

The Duster, now with 35 psi in its tires, began to show a new personality. At the end of the test Posey had revised his earlier opinion.

"Somehow, as the laps went by, this turned out to be the car that was a ball to drive. The steering is very, very light. Tremendous drift angles are possible, as are huge oversteers through the Esses with armloads of opposite lock. The car assumed nutty postures all the way around the course. It seemed to sort of get up on its tiptoes with the body rocking back and forth in a spectacular way and go really fast once I got used to it."

Of course, it still wasn't nearly as quick as the Chevelle, lapping at 1:11:7 and averaging 63.9 mph through the Hook and 60.2 through the Esses. But it was fun —a commodity that Posey didn't find much of in the Mustang.

"With the wide tires and stripes and louvers it looked so exciting in the pits. Perhaps because of my Trans-Am victory here in May with the Shelby car I had such high expectations for this one, but they just dwindled away as the laps went by. All I got out of it was sore hands. I'd rather just stand here and look at it."

At the beginning of the test we expected the Boss 302 to give the Cobra real chase, but with its 1:11:2 lap times it was only slightly quicker than the Duster. Of interest, however, was that its excellent transient handling made it only 0.3 mph slower through the Esses than the Chevelle.

With the Chevelle having established itself as the toughest of the Detroit representatives, the question now was how would it fare against the formidable Cobra. That confrontation could be put off no longer. Posey was already buckling himself into the cockpit.

"The most incredible feeling of immediacy exists in this car. Everything is up close to you. None of the remoteness found in the other cars. There was a feeling, in the others, that you had to penetrate the styling concepts to figure out which controls did what. Everything here is very obvious."

The Cobra is a shockingly single purpose car. No frills, no extra sound deadener, only the implements (tube frame, 4-wheel disc brakes, fully independent suspension) required for rapid transit. The flat instrument panel has simple, round, white-on-black gauges—one to monitor every factor you might need to check, including oil temperature. The external body sheetmetal extends right into the cockpit to form the top of the instrument panel and the windshield clamps down on the cowl, in traditional British sports car fashion, just inches in front of your nose. If there

is any doubt, at a skeletal 2322 pounds stuffed with a 271-hp Ford V-8, the Cobra is the archetypal high performance car.

"Oh, listen to the exhaust. If we were rating these cars on the basis of sound, this one would be the winner. The clutch is a heavy mutha. So is the steering, but it's very direct—much less lock required than in the other cars. And the suspension is very, very stiff. You feel *every* bump. Ah, see how nicely the tail comes out. This car has the feel of a racing car. The others didn't."

Because of its undisguised race car personality Posey adjusted to the Cobra in only a few laps. Partly because of its rearward weight bias—51.5% on the rear wheels—and partly because of its suspension rates, the Cobra was the only one of the cars that oversteered, and he used it to good advantage. In corners the Cobra adopted a curious posture. Because of its equal length arms, the independent suspension cambers the wheels in the same direction as body roll—which is exactly the wrong way. This, combined with the wide swinging tail, would have been humorous, except that the Cobra was ferociously eating up the circuit. Although the brakes began to fade after several laps the Cobra still made its point. With a best lap of 1:06:95 it was quicker than the Chevelle by slightly more than a full second. And, despite its suspension histrionics, the cornering speeds were faster too—by 2.5 mph in the Hook and 2.4 mph in the Esses.

Although lap times are a reliable indicator of a car's balance between handling and useful power, it doesn't tell the whole story about brakes, primarily because you never come to a complete stop on a road course. Fade and controllability of the braking process are measured but stopping ability is not. For that reason, the braking test had some interesting conclusions. The Cobra stopped quickest, requiring 256 feet (0.84G) from 80 mph. It was also the most controllable. The Chevelle was next at 272 feet (0.79G). Although it stopped in a straight line the braking was heavily biased toward the front wheels which meant that, to realize the full potential of the rears, the fronts had to be fully locked up, which will (and did) badly flat-spot the front tires. The Duster stopped in 287 feet (0.74G) with the rears tending to lock slightly before the fronts. The Mustang suffered from extreme rear wheel lock up—something that didn't show up significantly in the road course part of the test because a racing driver always avoids that situation if possible. Rear wheel lock up is a highly unstable situation which causes a car to skid sideways—which happened to the Mustang on one of its stops. Its best stop was 296 feet (0.72G)—an unseeming contrast to its stellar performance on the road course.

A point that Posey feels very strongly about, and so do we, is that controls, like brakes, should be sensitive to effort rather than travel. This problem shows up fre-

quently with the strong power assists that are necessary in Detroit's heavy cars. The Mustang's brakes are very good in this respect while the Chevelle's leave much room for improvement. And somewhat the same problem exists with power steering. The Duster's steering is so highly assisted that you sense the direction of the front wheels, not by feel, but by the position of the steering wheel.

After two solid days of testing we can see that improvement is required before Detroit can knock the Cobra off its "world's fastest car" pedestal—but not nearly as much as you may have thought. Those tweedy-capped purists who have been accusing Detroit's performance cars of being ill-handling hogs capable of little more than straight-line travel have had their legs kicked out from under them by the Chevelle. Naturally, the Chevelle was quicker in the straights, but it also made the fastest cornering speeds—significantly faster than the Boss 302—in fact, which has a reputation for good handling. After the test Posey commented on the Chevelle. "It's typically GM—wouldn't have offended anybody. It's quiet and well behaved—almost innocuous . . . I can't even remember what the dashboard looked like. But it has striking performance that you'd never suspect in traffic."

The Duster, although not the fastest, is certainly the most amusing. It's whimsical and has a kind of disposable air about it. Breaking, it would not be a catastrophe— you just won't get your deposit back. For the price it delivers a full measure of performance but it has been badly compromised by confused priorities (the shift linkage) and inept stylists. Not only are the stylists responsible for many unnecessarily cheap looking details in the interior (fake wood knob, for example), but by their decree the Duster has been lowered on its suspension. This little trick for snuggling the Duster down against the ground has left the suspension jounce travel in an impoverished condition, detrimental to both ride and handling. Still, the Duster is a good start toward a compact super car— the basic mechanical parts definitely do the job—and with some work could be every bit as satisfying as the Chevelle.

Most of the Boss 302's problems could be cured by power steering (which is available) and less understeer. After driving the prototype Boss in Dearborn last spring we thought Ford had finally cured the understeer problem but, apparently, we were wrong. With its strong styling and quality feel the Mustang is an appealing road car, but that is quite apart from the implication of "Boss."

For now Perkins can continue along carefree paths, snuffing Corvettes in gymkhanas and autocrosses, confident in the knowledge that his aluminum-bodied Anglo-American hand grenade has got Detroit pretty well covered. But he is definitely not as anxious for the 1971 Chevelle as we are. ●

# Exoticars

## AC COBRA
## IAN WEBB, JUST LOOKING, THANK YOU

Mister Editor Hill Sir is a man of pretty refined taste (it says here in the script), like he runs a blown three-litre Capri. And he looks down his nose at great big vulgarities like Cobras and all the other candidates for the Last of the Hairy Sports Cars title.

Me, my taste is kind of coarser. I don't mind them putting up a bit of a struggle, or making a lot of noise about it, or giving a bouncy ride.

So I actually enjoy the Cobra . . . in a way. At least I enjoyed *one* of the pair I've been driving. We'll come to the other one later.

But first the good news. The Cobra in question was nothing like the last to be made at the funny little AC factory at Thames Ditton, Surrey; it was produced well before 1968. Still, it was in like-new nick, virtually as it came off the workshop floor (production lines being unheard of at Thames D) and therefore highly representative of the species. Warts and all.

Basically the Cobra was unbelievably simple. It consisted of no more than a ladder-type chassis formed around a pair of bloody great tubes, a disc-braked wheel hung on at each corner by wishbones and coil springs and an open two-seat body in aluminium. That was AC's contribution. The power unit was a 289 Ford V8 giving 271bhp, all of which in a car weighing 21cwt felt adequate (in fact more than adequate, thank you, vicar), especially when it rained.

So basic was the Cobra that it came without side windows. OK, so what do you expect for a measly £2952? Glass? You got perspex, formed into a sidescreen that unclipped and stowed behind the seats when not wanted. By sliding the screen open you could reach in and open the door. Outside handles? You're kidding, of course.

The next thing lacking is seat adjustment. The seats themselves were really hip-huggy buckets but without any rake adjustments at all and next to no fore and aft travel.

The fascia looks like someone has picked up an armful of instruments and switches and just dumped them into the panel. After a while you figure out the location of the more important ones. And then it's time to quit stalling and start the engine. Because soft rubber mounts, sound padding and all that sort of pansy stuff don't figure in the Cobra scheme of things, the result can be startling. The V8

catches up and rumbles into a brisk tickover, making the car shake all over (could be a song title there, Colonel) with light vibrations. Also a lot of noise. Already, when the thing's only idling. . .

All right, ease it into first. Iffff I can get the clutch down. It's like a ton weight. And start away. First there's a clonk and a jerk as the multi-jointed, un-cushioned drive line takes up the slack like a goods train. Then you're on the move and the Cobra's beginning to feel like a powerful car. All right, a hairy one.

Kind of sneaky, too; every time you lift off at high speed the car does a disconcerting wiggle. At 100 or more that's no joke so it's back to the owner to enquire politely whether the car always does that. It seems that it doesn't and the trouble lies in the limited-slip diff. So out comes that unit and in goes a spare. Whereupon the Cobra feels fractionally slower. This apparently is because the new unit has a higher ratio, just taking the edge off acceleration but pushing the top speed up from 135 or so mph to nearer 150.

It's surprising just how little difference the higher gearing makes to acceleration. The twitchiness ruled out drag runs on the original diff but times taken with the higher one are probably only slightly lower, if only because you can hold on in first, second and third up to higher speeds.

Anyway, this was the result of the tests on the high ratio axle:

|  |  |
|---|---|
| 0–30mph | 2.9sec |
| 0–40mph | 3.5sec |
| 0–50mph | 4.8sec |
| 0–60mph | 6.0sec |
| 0–70mph | 7.9sec |
| 0–80mph | 10.2sec |
| 0–90mph | 13.5sec |
| 0–100mph | 16.4sec |
| 0–110mph | 21.5sec |
| 0–120mph | 28.2sec |

Eventually, using a Belgian autoroute, the maximum speed was cranked up to an unnerving 147mph. Unnerving because at that velocity the highly unaerodynamic car is under something less than full control. The front end lift means that the steering has negligible effect, even assuming that you wanted to steer anything but a straight line at that speed. You may remember AC making the national dailies back in the early 1960s with a Cobra test run at 190 down the M1 but that was with a decent body shape quite different to the production job's bluff, chubby form.

The noise, too, is unbelievable; like sitting in a corrugated iron shed while the 4.7-litre engine thunders away at 6000-plus rpm. The transmission yowls, the tyres rumble and the wind howls. Removing the hood, a DIY kit of fabric and frame that packs away in the tiny boot, reduces noise levels to the merely unbearable. But it brings along wind buffeting as a new problem. Then again, it keeps the car cool. Even on a chilly day there's so much heat pouring into the cockpit from engine, gearbox and exhausts that I was soon sweating freely from warmth as well as nerves. Funnily enough, if you find hot feet funny, the worst of the heat finds its way up through the pedals. . .

The reason for being in Belgium with the Cobra, apart from the fact that the Belgians don't mind you driving around at more than 70mph, was to try the car around the old Spa Francorchamps circuit. It's on public roads in the Ardennes and therefore permanently available to any ordinary mortal who happens to be passing. Some of the GeePee drivers, underpaid and overworked fellows that they are, reckon that Spa is too fast and not safe enough, which is why Belgian Grands Prix are now held on nice little slot car circuits. After trying Spa in the Cobra I reckon they might just have a point.

Starting out gingerly and getting progressively braver, it turned out that the Cobra was a mild understeerer, easily steered on the throttle and—thanks to relatively skinny tyres on six-inch rims—a doddle to set up in a good old fashioned drift with all four wheels sliding nicely. Mind you, there's none too much precision about the way the Cobra handles and you spend a good deal of the time twirling away at the steering. Then again, that's all part of the fun. The brakes were less enjoyable, calling for nearly as much effort as the clutch and being sadly in need of a generous shot of servo assistance. And the ride is joggly, bouncing, rough. Very bad for the bladder, old boy.

Still, on the open road the Cobra's a ball to drive. Around town, the heavy clutch and the cockpit heat make it something of a drag.

But if you can put up with that, and can stand fuel consumption of around 12-16mpg, this is another of those exoticars you can buy without robbing a bank first. Production stopped three years ago after about 1650 had been made and prices fell accordingly. They're starting to climb again now though less than two grand should buy a fair example of the 150-odd Cobras not exported to America. Service? Well, anything that US Ford and AC can't cope with should be mendable by the village blacksmith. It's that kind of car. Just don't be surprised if your insurance man pees himself when you whisper 'Cobra' down the phone.

Oh, and that other Cobra mentioned earlier? That was one of the very first examples, little more than an old 2-litre AC with a new 4.7-litre engine. The worst thing about it was that the suspension consisted of transverse leaf springs and lower wishbones, like a prewar Fiat 500. With that kind of power and *that* kind of suspension can you imagine how it handled?

## SPECIFICATION :

**Engine :** V8-cylinder water-cooled. Bore 101.6mm. Stroke 72.9mm. Capacity 4727cc. Compression ratio 11.1 to 1. One Holley four-barrel carburetter. Maximum power 271bhp at 5900rpm. Maximum torque 314 lb/ft at 3400rpm.
**Transmission :** Four - speed manual all-synchromesh.
**Suspension :** Front — independent by double wishbones and coil springs. Rear—independent by double wishbones, radius arms and coil springs.
**Steering :** Rack and pinion.
**Brakes :** Discs front and rear.
**Dimensions :** Length 13ft, width 5ft 8in, height 4ft 1in, wheelbase 7ft 6in, front track 4ft 6in, rear track 4ft 5in. Weight 21cwt.
**Price :** When new in 1968— £2952.

1966 A.C. Ford Cobra 427

THE AC ACE was originally designed to take 80 bhp or so from the old AC 2-litre engine. I have just been proving that what is recognizably the same vehicle can absorb over 500 bhp from a "hot" 7-litre Ford V8 engine, and that in this guise it is a superb touring car!

This car was one of a pair built for a wealthy American driver. The other one was purely a track car, but the present machine has all the road equipment of a standard 4.7-litre Cobra. However, the 7-litre engine has Shelby aluminium racing cylinder heads and it also has a "full race" bottom end, including special connecting rods at £30 each. It differs from the 550 bhp racing unit in having a gentler camshaft for road use, and in fact its characteristics are ideal, for it will creep through London traffic in top gear or, with a bellow of rage, swing the rev counter needle past 6000 rpm in the same gear in a few seconds—and that means 144 mph on the 3.54 to 1 rear end which is at present installed.

With all that torque available, normal tyres would be quite incapable of transmitting the power to the road. However, this is one of 50 special Cobras which were built to give body clearance for immense racing tyres on wide light-alloy wheels. These are almost unbelievably effective, and all the power can be used all the time, except from a standing start.

The present owner, John Woolfe, has had the car converted to right-hand drive. This is not supposed to be possible with the 7-litre engine, owing to the position of the starter motor, but some modification of the bulkhead and pedals has allowed the standard British steering gear to be adopted. An effective hood with detachable sticks came with the car, but to enjoy it to the full I drove the machine in open form.

Driven slowly, this Cobra seems a real heap! The huge tyres make the steering feel sloppy and the rear end kicks about over bumps, with apparently no directional stability at all. When one releases a few hundred horses, the car instantly comes alive. At 150 mph it runs absolutely straight and true with no correction from the driver, who can relax with one hand on the wheel. In spite of its short wheelbase and wide track it is well balanced on corners, accepting a great deal of power when leaving a bend without getting sideways. On the wide open spaces of Snetterton I was surprised at the cornering power and controllability.

The acceleration is simply tremendous, and bears no relationship to that of any other road-equipped car. It is not only that the Cobra is light and has 500 bhp but, even more important, all that power can be transmitted to the road. Any sports car that one happened to encounter could be

## JOHN BOLSTER tries

# A 7-litre AC Cobra

overtaken without bothering to change down.

My first attempt at the standing quarter-mile produced a time of 12.8 s which, with a little practice, I reduced to 12.4 s. This was achieved by using only moderate wheelspin at the start but keeping just appreciable wheelspin going for a considerable distance. It was found best to change up relatively early, employing no more than 6000 rpm on any gear, and I did not snatch the changes with an open throttle. The clutch is perfectly happy to handle all that torque and the gearbox gives light, fast changes. For my fastest standing quarter-mile I used top gear for quite a distance towards the end of the run. From a standing start, 100 mph comes up in 9.8 s, using the three lower gears.

With the special racing bottom end, the engine is safe up to 7000 rpm, but I am too much of a mechanical purist to let an engine with nearly a litre per cylinder run that fast. With a really wild camshaft, it might pay to use such extreme revs, but with a road camshaft there seems no reason to do so. The final drive ratio fitted suits the average circuit very well and gives an easy 150 mph without over-revving. With a higher gear (lower numerical ratio) and a hard top on the body, extremely high speeds would certainly be possible, but the present gear ratio is a very good compromise for normal use.

The car takes a bit of stopping from high speeds. The brakes are there all right,

and they do not fade, but a strong right leg is required for emergency retardation. However, when a corner rushed towards me and I realized that I had left it a bit late, my fear lent extra strength to my muscles and I did not enter the *décor*. A lady driver, for whom this car is otherwise perfectly suited, would want a bit more servo assistance on the pedal.

No better town and shopping car could be imagined. It is immaterial whether one uses first gear or third for starting from the traffic lights, as in either case the rest of the traffic just melts out of sight. The engine idles absurdly slowly and completely evenly, the typical V8 exhaust note smoothing out into quite a high-pitched scream as the big engine attains full revs. Apart from the exhaust, the engine is remarkably quiet mechanically and the gearbox and final drive are quite inaudible. At reasonably high speeds the ride is very comfortable, and the seats give good location. The handling is far better than that of other Cobras I have driven, the suspension obviously having been set up correctly for the enormous racing tyres. Unfortunately the stupendous performance must be paid for at the rate of 10 mpg or worse.

John Woolfe is very fond of his Cobra, as he has good reason to be. However, he is deeply involved in other racing projects and may find little time to make full use of this delightful machine. Anybody wishing to own a Lamborghini-eater might do worse than try tempting him with a cheque book.

# BEAUTY~OR A BEAST?

The AC Cobra 289 is the stuff of legends. Already a true classic, fetching inflated prices, its combination of American power with a traditional English chassis made it the most exciting sports car of the Sixties. Is it really as ferocious as it looks and sounds? To find out, Rex Greenslade tested two versions – a racer and a standard road car. His conclusions follow the colour section

# BEAUTY — OR A BEAST?
*continued*

I ONCE owned an AC. It was an Ace, 1962 vintage, fitted with a special AC engine, close ratio gearbox and painted a gorgeous maroon. I rebuilt it from the ground up and lavished care, hard work and money on it for 4½ idyllic years.

The love affair ceased in 1973 when I sold the Ace to go motor racing. I regret parting with the car even now. Not so much because the price I got then (£1,000) hardly reflects the value now (£4,000), more because losing it was like losing a friend. I have never become so attached to an inanimate object.

In all those years the one car I would have readily traded the Ace in for was a Cobra. But I had as much chance (as a 23-year-old) of obtaining insurance on that as on a submarine with a soft top. Now I've missed my chance and (unless you're extraordinarily rich) so have you too. Three years ago you could have obtained a tatty Cobra for about £4,000. Nowadays prices range from £10,000 to £35,000 for a fully restored 7-litre. Try justifying that to your accountant.

Of course you can't justify spending that sort of money to anyone but yourself. Yet people spend such sums, and I've a sneaking suspicion that if I were — eh — a lot better off than I am I'd probably be writing out a cheque right now. For having owned the next best thing to a Cobra, I am a completely unashamed Cobra fan, and if you're looking for a totally unbiased, objective assessment go no further. This isn't one.

But how could anything about Cobras be loaded with other than superlatives? As perhaps the fastest road car ever made in significant production numbers, the Cobra was for Men only. It thrilled anyone who drove it, enchanted many (hence the inflated prices!) and scared silly even more. It was once said by an American journalist, after watching a Cobra compete on a dragstrip: "Man, that car don't need no driver. All you need is someone to *steer*."

The Mk III 289 that *Motor* tested in October 1967 accelerated from 0 to 60 mph in 5.6 sec, from 0 to 100 mph in 13.7 sec and covered the standing ¼-mile in 14.4 sec. The ex-John Woolfe 7-litre car tuned to produce around 500 bhp — assessed by Roger Bell one month later in *Motor* — returned the staggering figures of 4.2, 10.3 and 12.4 sec respectively. That was fast enough to render some of our road test team speechless (it was rated as the world's easiest car to spin round its own gearlever) and faster than any other car that we tested for nearly a decade. Few of *Motor's* 1967 team are still with the magazine but mention the Woolfe Cobra to those that remain and they'll say (with a wink and a smile) "*That* Cobra!" and immediately break out in a cold sweat.

So it is not an understatement to say that the Cobra is a legend within *Motor* itself and I'm now one of the privileged few, having driven two:

Cornering styles track (above) and road (below). The racer demanded great respect, while the roadster could be slid through corners in a classic four-wheel drift

Spot the difference! The 'tame' Cobra is the one with the screen and number plates. It only races occasionally and it's only *very* fast, while the black one . . .

one on the road and the other on the track. It stemmed from an offer by Martin Colvill (of East Horsley's Bell and Colvill, East Horsley 4671) to drive his racing 4.7-litre Mk II. Having seen the beast in action once I didn't really fancy driving something quite that hairy, absolutely "cold". So Martin rustled up an absolutely standard Mk II from a friend, David Duffy, to drive up to Silverstone; a gentle baptism, so to speak.

A word about nomenclature here. A Mk I Cobra was essentially an Ace — complete with ladder-frame of 3in tube, worm and sector steering and transverse leaf springs — simply fitted with a 260 cu in Ford V8 engine. Essentially a feasibility study by Shelby and AC, the Mk I became the production Mk II with the adoption of rack and pinion steering and a 289 cu in (4.7-litre) V8. The Mk III had coil spring suspension, 4in chassis tubes more widely separated and the choice of a 427 cu in for the US (7-litre) or a 289 cu in for Europe (the so-called AC 289). A total of 1011 Cobras was made between 1962 and 1969; there are only about 86 in the UK, of which perhaps 50 are Mk IIs. As the 7-litre cars were intended for the US they are very rare in the UK and staggeringly valuable.

Duffy's has no particular history, having had four owners since new and as Duffy puts it: "The mileage of 57,000 is probably genuine. For although it was made in 1964 it was laid up for a number of years in the early '70s, during which time it had a botched up engine rebuild. So when I bought it 18 months ago it looked good but was very rough mechanically. So I've rebuilt the engine, brakes, most of the suspension, fitted a new clutch and rewired it."

As far as Cobras go this is a familiar story. It was between four and two years ago that most enthusiasts got their hands on the Cobras remaining and set about rectifying the misdemeanours and neglect of less conscientious previous owners; nowadays tatty Cobras aren't to be found. But in 1975 when Martin Colvill bought his, they were. It cost £3,500 and an almost incalculable amount of time and money has been spent restoring it, first as an immaculate concourse-standard road car, and then as one of the most beautiful classic sports car racers you'll ever see.

Martin never intended to make it

a racing car, but like Duffy (who competes in sprints and race meetings in his Cobra every other weekend during the summer), the call of the track proved irresistible. Cobras were never intended to be poodled along King's Road, they were meant to be driven, and driven *hard*. If doing that without falling foul of Her Majesty's servants means racing, then that's what a Cobra should do.

The fact that David Duffy's car is prepared solely by him and has proved totally reliable throughout hard usage speaks volumes for the car's basic concept and strength. If only such cars were made now... The specification is like a dream: 271 bhp (much more with tuning); around 19 cwt; close ratio gearbox; choice of six final drives; disc brakes all round...

The one extra that wasn't listed, but would have been useful, was a right ankle strap. Along bumpy, winding roads, the AC's ride becomes, shall we say, a little turbulent making it simply impossible to maintain a steady pressure on the accelerator. Try as you may, progress tends to be in a series of staccato bursts.

But of course that's half the fun. The Cobra is a car that improves vastly on acquaintance, and with my previous experience of an Ace breaking the ice, so to speak, took relatively little time. The resemblance to the Ace was quite uncanny — somehow Duffy's Cobra felt just like putting on an old suit of clothes. The facia was familiar, the overall feel (despite the heavier engine and different steering) almost identical. The massive bellhousing of the big V8 had made the footwell much more cramped, though, and the clutch was certainly heavier, if still extremely progressive.

Of course, the biggest difference lay in the performance. Using half throttle and, say 3000 rpm, the performance is electrifying enough. But with 6000 rpm and full throttle the urge is little short of breath-taking. Passing other road users is disdainfully easy; in the time it takes you to get past, they're still looking in the mirrors wondering where the hell you went.

On the road, performance of this magnitude is almost an embarrassment. Until you realise that the handling and roadholding are really quite respectable, you tend to blast up the straights and back off in a blue funk before the corners. You need to be very brave (or misguided) to explore the ultimate limits of a Cobra on the road. Suffice it to say, that at 100 mph the exhaust takes on a new, deeper, more purposeful note and the car feels as if it's only just getting into its stride.

A whole heap of horses. The standard 4.7 litre engine was quoted at 271 bhp (gross) and Martin Colvill's (below) produces in excess of 400...

I arrived at Silverstone exhilarated but nonetheless still uneasy. And when I saw Martin Colvill's black monster my apprehension increased. It looked so *evil*, so *threatening*. Enormous 8in rims hid beneath bulging wheelarches, and beneath the bonnet lay a collection of four twin-choke downdraught Webers like I'd never seen before. Around 400 bhp the man said. And I was supposed to *drive* it.

On a few occasions on the trip up I'd slid the road car's tail wide on a slow corner, and exited on a glorious touch of opposite lock. On one occasion I'd even managed a passable four wheel drift — though I wouldn't swear to it; it was so heart-stopping my mind nearly went blank. But I just couldn't conceive of being able to do the same with the Colvill beast. Suffice it to say that the other machine I was track testing the same day had more power, half the weight and wheels twice as wide (of which more soon); and I wasn't worried about driving that.

Apart from the obvious modifications mentioned above, a quick run-down with Martin revealed that he'd fitted some very stiff anti-roll bars front and rear, Spax dampers, Teflon bushes for the wishbones, and Dunlop CR 65 L/M section tyres — as required by the regulations, which in essence allow you to do anything as long as it had been done between 1960 and 1964. Hence Gurney-Weslake heads are out. But Martin's Mathwall-prepared engine boasts a steel crank, forged rods, full race heads and camshafts and a high performance J block. And a burstproof bell housing. Why? "The clutch/flywheel is very close to your

left foot." Umm.

They fired it up: that glorious V8 sound, woofly and off-beat on light throttle, cracking and barking when the accelerator was blipped. Just like the Le Mans GT40s, someone said. I began to sweat.

They fitted me into the cockpit: just like the road car really, and as Martin's 6 ft 5 in or so, I had no troubles in squeezing in, unlike many track test cars. There was a nice thick-rimmed wheel, and perfectly sited pedals. The clutch felt very heavy. My stomach began to heave.

They waved me off: down the pit road and up to Becketts, sounding all the world like an F5000 car. It slithered around a lot in those first few laps — tyre compounds were much harder in the '60s than they are nowadays. But the gearchange was magnificent (crisp, fast) and the engine simply glorious.

They called me into the pits: check over. I called Martin over. "This speedo isn't accurate, is it? I'm getting — er — 182 mph coming up to Woodcote." He laughed, which I took to mean it wasn't. "And the tyres, don't they take ages to warm up?" Martin: "Normally not more than about three laps at racing speed, though I must admit the rears get pretty hot at the start!"

They gave me the thumbs-up: out again. This time there was no time for pussy-footing; a Cobra needs to be shown who's boss. The first time I really booted it out of Becketts all hell let loose as the rear wheels scrabbled for grip. I backed off before I broke Silverstone's lap record in reverse. The next lap it was better, the one after that sensa-

tional. With the tyres hot, the Cobra turned into the corners much more responsively, and then progressive application of power turned the slight understeer into the classic four wheel drift, until as the machine drifted towards the edge of the tarmac the throttle could be floored, opposite lock wound on and two next black lines of rubber left for 30-odd yards on to the straight.

That was at Becketts, where there's plenty of room to spin harmlessly should you overdo it. My driving tactics were much more subdued through Woodcote and Copse. Cornering the beast through there at racing speeds requires far more acclimatisation and courage than I was able to call upon on the day. And in any case, it's very bad form to bend a machine on a track test. Especially one as valuable as the Colvill Cobra.

The big car's brakes were simply outstanding, not surprisingly since Martin Colvill has lavished money and development on them to ensure that his treasure stays on the track. The ventilated discs and four pot calipers worked superbly well, hauling the monster down to sensible speeds time after time with no hint of fade. Even Woodcote — my most un-favourite corner — was less horrific than I expected, despite the Cobra reaching about 150 mph by the end of the Club Straight.

We had hoped to record some standing starts with our fifth wheel equipment for it's only when you plant some black rubber on the tarmac and acrid rubber smoke fills the cockpit that you find out how staggeringly fast a racing Cobra is. But it wasn't possible. Some other time, perhaps.

Much of the restoration work on Martin's car was completed by Autokraft of Brooklands (Weybridge 40049) who now hold all the original AC body jigs. Boss Brian Angliss even owns the full race sister car to the Woolfe 7-litre monster that *Motor* tested in '67. If your appetite has been whetted, like mine, let me let you into a secret. He's currently manufacturing 40 replica 7-litres absolutely from scratch. Of course they can't be called ACs, but they'll be virtually indistinguishable from the real thing. There's one problem. Every single one is going to North America. But if you ask Brian nicely, maybe...

Perhaps you'd prefer the real thing, though. And Bell and Colvill might (only might, I must accentuate) be able to help you out. As dealers in Maserati, Alfa Romeo, Lotus and AC, Cobras do pass through their hands once in a while.

The question is: could you afford one?

# States-side Stallion

**The Cobra's legend lives on in this Californian glass-fibre replica of the sixties classic. Howard Walker reports**

FEW CARS have ever caused so much adrenalin to flow as the legendary AC Cobra — to label its performance as "breathtaking" must rate as one of the understatements of all time.

To the fortunate few who ever got to grips with this slingshot it was an experience never to forget, the idea alone of up to 7-litres of American Ford V8 clothed in a wafer thin aluminium body would bring a smile to the lips of any enthusiast.

The Mk III 289 tested by *Motor* back in 1967 sprinted from standstill to 60 mph in just 5.6 sec and reached 100 mph in 13.7 sec — performance indeed.

But all too few of the cars were built by the Thames Ditton company and with the inevitably high number of accidents caused by too much power and too little experience, there are few cars which remain and the ones that do command prices of anything up to £35,000.

On the other side of the Atlantic, the Cobra has become a collector's classic with wealthy enthusiasts queuing to join the cult and for this reason alone a number of specialist companies have built glossy replicas — the latest comes from the Californian company Red Stallion.

The company is run by ex-book salesman Jim Kellison who before his literary exploits raced sports cars for nearly 15 years. His Cobra replica, named the Stallion, more resembles the 'sixties classic than faithfully reproduces it.

Instead of aluminium, the body shell is moulded in glassfibre and formed in a rotary mould allowing it to be produced in one piece. This is then bolted on a tubular space-frame chassis which has a monocoque backbone of two sheets of 20-gauge steel sandwiching a slab of foam. The main frame members are hefty 3in × 4in flat-sided tubing.

Red Stallion say that great emphasis has been placed on passenger safety with the cockpit being essentially a "cocoon of steel" with tubing and glassfibre sandwiched between steel plate. The 18-gallon fuel tank is enclosed in an 18-gauge sheet-steel liner but rather dubiously, is bolted to glassfibre with the idea of letting it move without rupturing.

The front suspension has upper and lower wishbones with coil springs and heavy duty racing shock absorbers. At the rear there is a live axle sprung by coils and located by four links. Ventilated discs at the front and 11-in finned drums at the rear provide the braking.

There's a choice of engines ranging from 5-litre Ford 302 V8 to the huge 8-litre 460 V8. Even in 302 form the Stallion is claimed to have "shattering" acceleration.

Steering is by rack and pinion with an option of power-assistance. And there's also the choice between manual and automatic transmission. The heavy duty alloy wheels are built by Ford's Lincoln division with 7in × 15in front rims and 10in × 15in at the rear.

As you would expect this American sportster is far from spartan with plush carpeting throughout, a thickly padded facia, a stereo radio and cassette player, a tinted windscreen and padded cockpit surround. And, of course, there is plenty of brightwork with chromed side exhausts, roll-over bar, racing type petrol filler cap and optional chromed wire wheels. If that doesn't make the Stallion glitter then the 40 coats of acrylic paint and two coats of lacquer will.

In its basic form the car costs well over £17,000 in California and when you have added the price of the little extras like Connolly leather upholstery, air conditioning, power steering, a limited slip differential, a tonneau cover and wire wheels you are talking about £20,000.

For a Stallion built with reconditioned parts the cost is slightly less but still well over £13,000. In a rolling chassis form without an engine, gearbox, paintwork or battery the cost is a mere £9,000.

As yet there is no indication as to whether the Stallion will reach Britain but I feel it is unlikely. If it managed to pass our stringent safety tests the cost of importing it would make the Stallion's price tag astronomical — probably more than an original Cobra at present prices.

Cobra replicas are nothing new. Brian Angliss, at CP Autocraft in Weybridge, has not only built up virtually new cars from write-offs but he has exported to America a number of aluminium replicas based on the Cobra.

With the shortage of Cobras in the United States there is little doubt that the Stallion, which is only destined to be produced in a limited edition, will be in demand. Whether it has the bite of the original Cobra is a different matter.

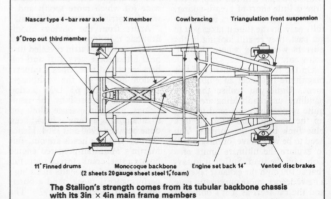

The Stallion's strength comes from its tubular backbone chassis with its 3in × 4in main frame members

It's still got that Cobra look from this angle, a view that few see unless the car is parked!

# METAMORPHOSIS OF A COBRA

## *The Cobra Sheds Its Skin And We Find A Stallion*

### Photos and Story by Dennis Adler

The AC Cobra lives! That was our first impression when Silver Classic Coachcraft delivered its 1979 Stallion 429 to our doorstep for evaluation.

The Cobra image rapidly diminished as our inspection uncovered very little of the AC remaining in the Stallion. In fact, the only trace of Cobra to endure was the windshield. Every other facet of the car had been altered.

This is not a critique of a poor copy, but, in fact, applause for a new automobile. The design changes from Cobra to Stallion are what chief designer Jim Kellison calls, "What the Cobra would be it it were designed today."

This new car is wider, longer, more spacious (someone 6'2" can actually get into the cockpit), and aerodynamically it is advanced over its 1962 predecessor. (Improving on near perfection. . .is that one-upmanship on a grand scale?)

The fiberglass body conceals a modern concept in automotive chassis design. Perhaps not new to the professional racing scene, but certainly new to the production car field. The Stallion is designed to go beyond mere street car driving. This car is built to race, if you are so inclined, and features designed for the track make the Stallion that much better on the street. This could be the safest sports car in America.

The Stallion is available with a choice of several engine/transmission combinations, most popular being the Ford 5.0 liter (302 c.i.d. V-8) with C-4 automatic transmission. Other combinations include the 302 with a manual four-speed top-loaded box, 351 Cleveland with C-4 automatic and a limited quantity of 400 c.i.d. V-8s with C-6 transmission. (This is the car we tested.)

Far beyond the myriad engine/transmission selections is the car's structural integrity. Here we see a prac-

tical application of race car technology brought forth into street car design. The Stallion is built on a tubular steel frame with monocoque backbone and a series of crash safety features. The front suspension (main frame rail) splits (see diagrams) into a configuration called redundant triangulation, resulting in a front end designed to crush (controlled crushability) under an impact of 30 mph, absorbing the collision inertia before it reaches the main frame rails and the engine. This affords considerable protection to the driver and passenger.

Safety is a major area of consideration in the Stallion. The car has two firewalls, one fore and one aft of the passenger compartment, the aft wall separating the cockpit from the fuel tank. Additionally, the entire passenger compartment is surrounded by steel framework attached to the chassis and frame. Closing the doors, which are

*CAR COLLECTOR*

Wider fenders and cockpit are evident in this view of Stallion.

Completed chassis, less body, with 429 Ford V-8.

The black body has just been removed from the mold while the gray body is in the process of being detailed out. The unique four-section mold used by Stallion produces a one-piece body unit.

Passenger's side of cockpit shows partly-finished chassis. Notice the construction of the firewall and backbone. The engine compartment side has been sealed off with the first of two sheets of 20-gauge steel. The cavities are filled with one inch of foam insulation, after which the second sheet of steel is welded in place.

Mike Grant, one of the design engineers, puts the Stallion through its paces on a Southern California back road.

hinged to the main chassis, completes a circle of steel. Each door, weighing 70 pounds, is steel-reinforced for side-crash protection and closes into a 3,000 pound-test lock which is also mounted to the frame, rather than the fiberglass body.

Crashing in an open roadster is perhaps one of the most feared of all motoring accidents, yet the Stallion is designed to withstand crashes that many production cars could not.

The fuel tank, or in this case, fuel cell, is a NASCAR bladder encased in an 18-gauge steel compartment mounted over the rear axle and protected from all sides. From above, the fuel cell is covered by the steel roll-bar, which is mounted in 1/8-inch steel cups and gusseted by ¼-inch steel plate. The spare tire compartment rests on the rear frame member which is designed to collapse inward and below the fuel cell in the event of a severe rear impact.

And, as mentioned earlier, there is a rear firewall between the cockpit and the fuel cell which, perhaps, offers the safest passenger/fuel risk factor available.

## COMFORT AND HANDLING

This is where all the research and design meet the man. Comfort is designed into the Stallion in less obvious ways. The dash is simple in design. There are no rare imported woods or fancy gauges here, only form-follows-function practicality. All the pertinent information is available to the driver at a glance. Seating is probably one of the key areas of driver comfort. No matter how beautiful the interior may be, if the driver has an uncomfortable understanding (pardon the pun) with the seat, even one finished with Connolly hides, he is most likely to feel ill at ease. This is not the case here. Stallion incor-

porates specially designed aircraft-type seats that give proper lumbar support and added lift in the thigh area of the cushion, thus supporting the body away from the spine and lessening the pressure in that area which causes driver backache.

Our full day's test drive, although exhausting, did not leave us heading for the whirlpool, as so many other less comfortable cars have. Our test vehicle sported the rare 400 cid V-8 with C-6 automatic transmission and power steering. Our first serious criticism is of the power steering which, as an option, we feel is more of a deficit than an assist. It takes away far too much of the road-feel necessary for a car with the Stallion's power.

Power again is another area that falls under the gun, but only if you have had the thrill of driving an original Cobra. The horsepower in the Stallion falls short of the AC version, but all things

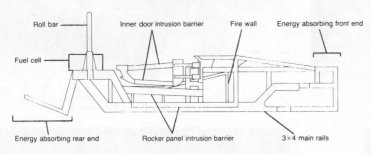

## STALLION FRAME SPECIFICATIONS

The Stallion chassis is a tubular steel space frame of parallel ladder design. The 3"×4"×.120" wall rectangular tube main frame supports a full monocoque backbone with the firewall and drive line tunnel built of two sheets of 20 gauge steel spot welded to the tube steel backbone. Sound deadening and heat protection is provided by slabs of polyurethane foam set between the 20 gauge steel plates. This, and the steel inner lines of the doors, encases the cockpit in a veritable cocoon of steel.

The angles on the frame are designed so that the front and rear frame tubes will break away and collapse sequentially on impact. The engine sits 14" back of the front axle, allowing the whole front end of the frame and the tires to absorb crash impact before the engine is reached. The design has been carefully calculated so that the car can absorb a tremendous impact without serious injury to the driver.

### CHASSIS SIDE VIEW

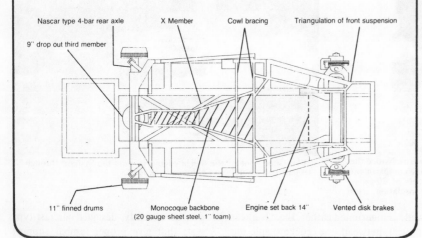

Roll bar — Inner door intrusion barrier — Fire wall — Energy absorbing front end

Fuel cell

Energy absorbing rear end — Rocker panel intrusion barrier — 3×4 main rails

### CHASSIS TOP VIEW

Nascar type 4-bar rear axle — X Member — Cowl bracing — Triangulation of front suspension

9" drop out third member

11" finned drums — Monocoque backbone (20 gauge sheet steel, 1" foam) — Engine set back 14" — Vented disk brakes

**Although it has little of the Cobra left in it, the Stallion still reflects that classy AC look.**

considered, unless you are planning an SCCA tour, the Stallion provides more than enough thrills for your speed dollar. Quietly cruising along at 60 mph we went to pass a Trans-am and found ourselves doing a respectable 100 mph in less than four seconds!

The suspension draws once again on race car design. It incorporates a Ford crossmember into the chassis itself, with fully independent A-arms, lower trailing arms, coil springs, anti-roll bar and Monroe heavy duty shocks on the front. The rear suspension is a NASCAR type (live rear axle) with four bar triangulated trailing arms, coil springs, anti-roll bar and the Monroe shocks.

The live rear axle might seem a little out of place in a car that has seen such design refinements, but considering the Stallion is almost entirely Ford components and since Ford does not manufacture an independent rear suspension, the use of the live rear is not so much *choice* as *availability*.

## THE FINISHING TOUCHES

The Stallion is unique in that, unlike many fiberglass bodies that are molded in sections and bolted to the frame, it is formed in a rotary mold made up of four units that produce a one-piece body.

After the initial fiberglass has been sprayed into the mold (a 1/16-inch base coat), two-ounce mat is hand-laminated around the seat buckets, headlight buckets, door seals, wheel wells and dashboard. The base coat is then sanded and ¼-inch more of glass is shot in. In addition, ½-inch nylon rope is dipped in resin and hand-laminated into all stress points that are not physically tied into the chassis, i.e. inside fender wells, around the hood, engine compartment rim, etc.

The entire body is coated with a two-component urethane-based primer and is then covered with two gallons of acrylic lacquer which is hand-sanded and finished with eight coats of clear acrylic. The frame if also treated and sprayed with two coats of black epoxy paint to reduce the chances of rust caused by water, road salts and assorted highway dirt. The chassis also has an oil vapor sealed inside the tubes before they are epoxied.

Unlike conventional cars, which have

an electrical system governed by fuses, the Stallion's electronics are controlled by circuit-breakers located beneath the dash. In the event of a short, you can trace the problem right to its source. (I wonder if you can put a penny in the fuse box?)

Overall, Silver Classic Coachcraft, Jim Kellison, and his creative staff totaling 35 people have spent years producing what they feel is the best sports car manufactured in America today. Whether that claim is well founded, only the test of time will tell!

*Editor's Note: Dennis Adler, a native of Palm Springs, California, is an alumnus of Los Angeles Valley College and also College of the Desert, where he majored in photo-journalism and won the Journalism Association of Junior Colleges' top journalistic award in 1968. He has been a free-lance journalist for the past fifteen years, (specializing in advertising public relations for the automotive industry), with two years time out in the Air Force where he was a public relations officer in the Strategic Air Command. Since then he has served as editor of* Custom Vans *magazine, associate editor of* Car Classics *magazine, and is presently associate editor of* Four Wheeler *magazine, as well as our own West Coast Editor. Dennis and his wife live in suburban Sherman Oaks, California.*

## STALLION 429 SPECIFICATIONS – 302 V-8

| | |
|---|---|
| Price as tested (with 400 cid V-8) | $30,000 |
| Curb weight, lb. | 2459 |
| Wheelbase, in. | 96 |
| Track, front/rear | 59/65 |
| Length, in. | 156 |
| Width, in. | 75 |
| Fuel capacity, U.S. gal. | 18 |
| Engine | Ford ohv V-8 |
| Bore x Stroke, in. | 3.0 x 4.0 |
| Displacement, cc/cid | 4940/302 |
| Compression ratio. | 8.0:1 |
| Torque, SAE net | 257 ft. lb. @ 2400 rpm |
| Power, SAE net | 152 bhp @ 2400 rpm |
| Final drive ratio | 2.75:1 (automatic C-4 transmission) 3.0:1 (four-speed manual transmission) |
| Carburetion | One 2 bbl. Motor Craft |
| Brake system | 9 in. ventilated disc, front – 11 in. finned drums, rear) |
| Chassis | Tubular steel space frame with monocoque backbone |
| Wheels | 7x15 front, 10x15 rear |
| Tires | E60–15 front, L50–15 rear |
| Steering | Rack and pinion (optional power steering) |
| Front suspension | Independent A-arms, lower trailing arms, coil springs, tube shocks, anti-roll bar |
| Rear suspension | NASCAR-type four-bar triangulated trailing arms, coil springs, tubular shocks, anti-roll bar |

# The Brute is back

It looks like a Cobra, it carries real AC badges and it's made in Britain by Autokraft. Roger Bell reports on the return of a sports classic

'Rows of brand-new AC Cobras in various stages of completion...' The scene recently at Autokraft.

'AC grant to Autokraft on an exclusive basis authority and licence during the period of this agreement to utilise and exploit . . . the use of the trademark AC'. In that snippet from an historic contract, signed last month, you have the nub of the matter — the rebirth of one of the world's most famous and covetted classics, the AC Cobra, built by Autokraft bearing the AC badge. Legally speaking, it is actually not a Cobra because Ford of America now own that evocative name and it would need the consent of the US giant (which might be forthcoming) to complete the famous nomenclature. But it's the use of the proper AC badge, available for 'Cobra-shaped cars' to Autokraft for the next 25 years, that sets the new Autokraft AC aside from all the other Cobra clones and replicas. That, and the way it's designed and built not only faithfully to capture the shape and spirit of the original, but also to satisfy American type-approval regulations. Initially, the first batch of 30 cars is destined for the States (they're being built with American money) where they will be sold with the approval of the authorities for what they are — brand new cars, not regulation-beating rebuilds.

Home of the Autokraft AC is not Thames Ditton but the Brooklands Industrial Estate, strong on motoring history but decidedly low on industrial glamour. The building is one of those dreary utilitarian blocks, and the small nameplate over the door is more to identify the place for deliveries than to attract customers. Stepping through the tin door of this unpromising abode, though, is like entering Aladdin's Cave. It's an amazing sight. There ahead of you are rows of brand-new AC Cobras in various stages of completion. The piercing clatter of panel beaters' hammers emphasises that you've not so much stumbled on buried trove as treasure in being made.

For Brian Angliss, one of the key men behind this million-dollar venture, it's just reward for the effort that he and his talented team have put into establishing Autokraft as one of the top specialist builders in the country. Angliss first constructed an AC replica in 1974, copying the chassis of a friend after AC had rejected his request to sell him one. That exercise led to Cobra Parts, then based at Chessington, later to become Autokraft at Brooklands. The spares and rebuild service will not be affected by Autokraft's new status of car manufacturer, incidentally. "Probably 60% of all ACs in the States now use our parts" says Angliss, who also supplies 'rival' Cobra replica builders, including Aurora and ERA Autos. Restorations and conversions will not be curtailed either: during our visit, we saw a Cobra powered by one of the rare 600bhp 7-litre overhead cam Ford engines under construction for a German customer, and a new thin-tube chassis being made for a 289. Nostalgia's twin turbocharged 7-litre Cobra, one of the stars of the Brighton Classic Car Show, was also prepared at Autokraft, though the general restoration business (where Rod Leach's Nostalgia car still resides) is now a separate enterprise, run by Emilo Garcia.

Such was Autokraft's standing in America that in 1978 Angliss was approached by Chicago businessman and enthusiast Richard Buxbaum to build a series of new Cobras for sale in the States. Buxbaum was not the first American to make such a proposal, but he *was* the first to support it with a contract and hard cash. The first car, virtually an exact copy of the real thing, was jigged around a '427' with a body made on AC's original wooden formers, now on permanent loan to Autokraft. Over the years, AC's Derek Hurlock evidently warmed to Angliss and the high quality of his work at Brooklands, appointing Autokraft as sole suppliers of genuine replacement AC bodies and panels some time ago.

Unfortunately, the first unmodified Cobra replicas did not conform to US type-approval regulations and were rejected by the authorities. Undaunted, Autokraft undertook a tedious and costly development programme designed to ensure that the cars *did* comply with American rules, including its stringent crash tests. 'We knew the original car was basically strong enough' says Angliss. 'And that the suspension worked well. So we retained the massive twin-tube chassis, its pickup points and original suspension components (all unique to the Cobra incidentally), and developed an entirely new superstructure for it. All we had to do then was drop in a type-approved engine, with full emission control.'

Angliss makes it sound easy but for a small concern like Autokraft to get a 'new' car through the US rulebook was a fine achievement. The tubular steel bumpers, for instance, *look* like the real thing, but are in fact mounted on hydraulic rams that telescope three inches into the chassis tubes on impact; the aluminium-skinned doors are reinforced for side-crash protection; and the 18-gallon fuel tank has been moved away from the tail to a safer place behind the cockpit.

Apart from proprietary running gear — Ford's 5.7 litre 351 'Windsor' V8, four-speed Borg Warner Super T10 manual gearbox (the one with steel casing and nickel-chrome gears), Salisbury (Jaguar XJ) final drive, and bought-out ancillaries like the Smiths instruments and heater (Triumph Dolomite), Autokraft make and assemble practically the entire car themselves. This includes not just the tubular-steel chassis and hand-shaped and welded aluminium body, but also the forged suspension uprights, hub carriers and wishbones, the specially-cast brake solid discs (clamped by Girling calipers), seatframes, brass screen surround, trim panels, wiring loom and many other vital parts. The car is also painted by Autokraft (they use nitro-cellulose that's force-dried in their own paintshop) and exquisitely trimmed by them too in Connolly hide. There are former Mulliner and Panther personnel among Autokraft's 30-strong team of skilled craftsmen and technicians whose standard of workmanship is of the very highest order. One of the few tasks they don't perform is to install the de-toxed Ford V8 engine which will be fitted in the States to save unnecessary freight charges.

To improve the car's finish, habitability and weatherproofing, four main glassfibre mouldings are placed between the bolted-together body and chassis. The biggest is that for the centre bulkhead which incorporates the footwells (deeper than the original's), transmission tunnel cover and heater ducting. Others are used in the fully trimmed boot and as underwing liners to protect the aluminium outer skin from stone dents. Compared with the original, there's more leg and elbow room — and considerably more plush — in the extended cockpit which will comfortably accommodate a 6ft 6in driver behind a steering wheel that's adjustable for reach as well as rake. "What we've done" says Angliss "is to develop the car as AC would have needed to do had it remained in production." It's in effect a Cobra Mk4, though what the Americans will call it has yet to be decided.

Whatever the nomenclature, it's a worthy successor to the last AC-built 'Cobra-shaped' car, if not quite such a potent one: nothing saps power quite so much as emission control equipment. Even so, with 170bhp to propel a car weighing around a ton, performance is still formidable, especially for America's speed-restricted roads. What owners do after purchase to extract even greater performance is their responsibility, not Autokraft's or that of their American associates. Running on huge Pirelli P7 tyres (255/60 at the front, 275/55 at the back) carried on 9½-inch wide wheels cast from an original Halli-brand mould, the car can certainly handle more power. Prices have yet to be fixed but they will inevitably be high, and there's the possibility of a re-engined version for Europe later. ⬣

**Above right, the cockpit is roomier than that of the original and trimmed in Connolly hide. Right, there'll be less air under the wings when the engine and gearbox are installed in the States.**

# BRIEF ENCOUNTER

**Mike Taylor and the Editor discover a small building on the edge of the Brooklands track where genuine A.C. sportscars are now being built the way they used to be...and become the first to drive a new A.C.**

**Y**OU can not help but admiring Brian Angliss. He has built up a small sportscar factory that has nothing to do with the 'replica' industry, his is the 'real thing'. He produces *official* A.C. sportscars, on original A.C. wooden bucks and with much equipment, craftsmen and know-how from A.C.

Walk around his tiny factory and you quickly appreciate that he has established a Morgan-style operation, but has set about it in a way that out-Morgans Morgan. For the entire car is built up, there is not even a bought-in chassis.

All around you are craftsmen, rolling by hand sheets of alloy or welding up chassis tubes like birdcages fit for an Albatross.

It's an amazing sight. Here is a tiny time-capsule, using very traditional methods of sportscar build. The result is an accurate but imporved-upon official Mark Four of the A.C. that is now fondly regarded as THE hairy-chested sportscar of the 1960s.

The latest version is a lot less hairy, much more suited to present motoring

conditions, and spits a good deal less venom than the Cobras of old. "That's because I wanted a car which anyone's girlfriend could drive. I wanted a very quick A.C., but also a sportscar which is versatile for 1980s motoring," explained Angliss. The six-litre Ford ironblock V8 is hardly stressed at all with just 200bhp, due to all the antismog gear on the car we drove before it was shipped to America.

But it is nonetheless a very exhilerating car. Open the door, and you notice the attention to detail, for this is no single piece of aluminium on a couple of rabbit-

hutch hinges, you have to really tug it open because the door fits so well. Its surprisingly weighty too, containing a steel bar for side-crash protection, part of the way the original A.C. has been updated to successfully meet all the Type Approval safety legislation for export. The interior is beautifully appointed in cream hide, even the inside of the door is now trimmed in hide, a far cry from the days of a strip of sticky Fablon over bare tin.

Slip inside, legs clearing the woodrim wheel with ease, find the pedals, over there, well to the left, what a lot of offset.

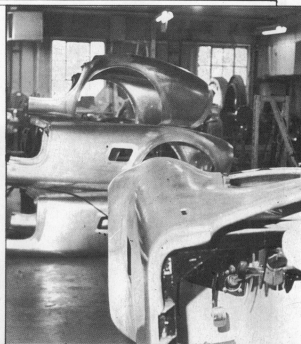

Get comfortable. The seat back is good, made just like the original thing of the 1960s, but there is precious little side support, you feel as if you are sitting on it, not in it, the squab could be longer, isn't new leather slippery? Find the key. Everything is phallic about this car... its between your legs, grope under the steering column, give it a turn. A deep gruff growl, turns into tick-over of burble-waffle-burble-waffle, V8 double-beat.

Black-faced instruments set deep into cream leather-padded dash suggest all is well, temperatures rise. The Borg-Warner box has that typically American chrome lever, but it moves into first with little movement, but the clutch is very firm perhaps not as heavy as a Morgan, and the steering at first takes some effort to twitch those massive wheels that really do need those aggressive flares in the wings to cover 255-section 15-inch Pirelli P7s. (Even wider at the rear).

It's a rack-and-pinion set up, very accurate, with 3.3 turns lock to lock as opposed to the old 2.9 gearing, again a modification to suit current motoring.

Vision down that beautifully curving bonnet is superb, the burbling note rises, and its off, no dramas, no wheelspin no macho-sounding screech of tyres, it is all so remarkably tractable you wonder if its in fourth gear by mistake. Give it some right foot, and it stops pottering along, acceleration produces a truly neck-snapping shove.

Away! Into second, past 60mph, the road across the Brooklands airfield enters the start of an open 'S' bend that gradually tightens up, back off, trailing throttle, the track is very damp, lets be

careful. Goodness, it understeers like, well a De Haviland Chipmunk, Hell... It runs wider and wider, sweeps through the bend, coming out power is applied early and right away the steering lightens, response is immediate. The car tucks in at the front, the rear squats down and moves very slightly sideways, enough to cancel all that tugging understeer. It offers bags of feel.

Now you are getting the hang of it, this needs to be accelerated through corners, but having been set up carefully to sart with; here's another corner, the brakes seem a little soft, with so much servo assistance a smaller-sized master-cylinder could. be the answer, but with so much rubber the A.C.s claws into the ground, now it.can turn into the corner with a dab of throttle. Not too much!

The independent rear suspension is excellent over the potholes and broken tarmac, without a trace of shudder or banging around, it doesn't seem to flex much and is commendable ˙aut-feeling. And no rattles. The rear of the car seems surprisingly soft, for a hairshirt sports car its ride gives unexpected degrees of suppleness.

The finish is something everyone at Autokraft takes a pride in, and the quality of the paint, the way things fit together, and the interior, are all very much improved on the A.C. of the 1960s. It will be a success in America, that is for sure, and Brian Angliss now hopes to establish sales in Britain, and is looking for dealer outlets.

It's a far cry from the days when he first started, with just a small A.C. repair shop. He began by restoring a crashed seven-litre Cobra, took the measurements

to help him build himself another car, and started to gain a reputation, with requests coming from America for spares. Cobra Parts were now in business. Anyone with a genuine log-book from an A.C. could have a car made. He shunned publicity and operated behind Box Numbers and ex-directory telephone numbers, but still people sought him out. He still is not keen on publicity — we failed to persuade him to be photographed. But to just have Graham Murrell (who is the official photographer to the A.C. club as well as being photographer of *Sporting Cars*) to take pictures behind his closed doors was a privilege as far as we were concerned.

Even with all its smog gear, the strangled V8 is good for around 130mph and will shift the one-ton A.C. to 60mph in around seven seconds on its Salisbury diff with 3.3 ratio. Coming soon for Britain: The Ford engine without all the power-sapping additions, opening up more bhp and even more massive amounts of torque, combined with a five-speed gearbox, and Salisbury diff with lower gearing of 3.5 to improve the punch still further.

"They like it," said Brian Angliss, "I have worked very closely with the Hurlocks and the A.C. factory for a number of years. What they had around is now here, like the wooden forms for bodywork, even the forgings for the making of A.C. suspension wishbones, which we have strengthened, jigs, dies, drawings, and men who knew the car, it is a real A.C., and is officially registered as an A.C. Mark Four. Ford of America have the Cobra name, but I'm working to get it."

With the A.C. factory now selling its stock of mid-engined 3000ME, with production men laid off, it could be a sad fact of life that the famous name of A.C., which has been one of the World's oldest sportscar names, could now rest on the operation that has been set up to recreate the British supercar of the 1960s.

Should not A.C. have done it? "That's difficult," said Angliss. "They have always looked forward, not backward. Would Morgan be making something with running boards if they had successfully moved on to a modern-concept sportscar? I doubt it. Could you say to Jaguar, or Aston Martin, why not turn out a new D-Type, or DB3S? Would Colin Chapman look backwards to the old Elite, if he went through a difficult spell? No.

"It is easier for someone else to come along and say, by all means keep looking forward, but can I please have your Blessing to produce the masterpiece you dropped yesterday? Even then it's not easy!"

A stroke of good fortune for Brian was an American who was so keen to help that he paid all the development costs to meet Type Approval legislation for the States. And when he talked of dropping in the (ex-Buick) Rover V8, he received a phone call from America that went something like this:

"Hi! Is that Brian Angliss?" Yes. "Hi! This is Ford of America! We've been reading all about you over here, good job you're doing, lad!" Thanks. "Now what in Hells name is all this about you going for that Rover engine? Hell man, that ain't original, our rival mob were throwing that thing away, when the Brits

picked it up. Tell you what, why don't we supply you with real V8s?" Oh Really? I didn't think you would be interested.

End of conversation — Ford started to supply. The car we test drove was on its way to Karl Ludwigson, top brass at Ford.

The Cobra chassis was tuned by computers of Ford of Dearborn in the 1960s, and was considerably improved upon with the resources of Ford, who took to the car in a way not seen by a big manufacturer since Len Lord of BMC brought Donald Healey under his wing.

(Healey would still be making cars today if he had said no to Lord, but that's another story).

Brian Angliss has a liking for many sportscars, he's worked on GT40s, he has produced a Spyder conversion of half a dozen Ferrari Daytonas, but he's a British sportscar fan at heart. He is an avid Bentley enthusiast and owns an ex-Brooklands Bentley.

Said Angliss: "One day, Victor Gauntlett will drop in for a chat, and of course if he ever does I would like to think that even he with his Aston Martin standards

will find a lot to admire in our workmanship." If he ever does, I said, he would probably ask for a tape measure — to see if an Aston engine would drop into your enginebay! Brian smiled.

"No, we would go away and sit in a quiet corner...and talk Bentleys."  ☐

*Pictures by Graham Murrell show the inside of C. P. Autokraft at Byfleet. Here seats receive final stitching, alloy wings rolled by hand, chassis welding...its all under one roof, and all craftsman made like AC's of old.*

# COBRA REPLICAS

*The ultimate do-it-yourself performance kits*

**BY TONY HOGG**

IT APPEARS THAT the decade of the Eighties is turning into the decade of the replicas because one sees them on the streets in every shape, size and form and they are widely advertised in kits, partially assembled kits or as complete cars. Actually, this has been going on for a long time, but only recently has it really blossomed. Among the many replicas available are about eight versions of the Cobra, so we rented Riverside International Raceway for a day and assembled two of the better known and established replicas plus an original to use as a benchmark. We also asked Carroll Shelby, who after all was the instigator of the whole thing, to come along to comment, which he did.

The two replicas we selected were the ERA made by ERA Replica Automobiles of New Britain, Connecticut and the Contemporary Cobra Replica made by Contemporary Classic Motor Car Co Inc, Mount Vernon, New York. The reason for selecting these two is that both companies have sold quite a number of cars and the cars themselves seem to be well engineered.

The trouble with the replica business is that it tends to attract a variety of people. Some are on an ego trip, some are sincere, honest and well intentioned, but many of them have no conception of the amount of financing involved. And then there are a few who have a roguish trend, but there is always a bad apple in every barrel. It is for these reasons that we at *Road & Track* have been somewhat cautious in our coverage of replicas.

Many of the kit cars and replicas of all kinds on the road never cease to amaze me, not only because some of them are incredibly ugly, but also because they are complicated and expensive to build. In the case of the fiberglass Cobra replicas, this is not true because the body is relatively easy to produce and it is one of those timeless designs that will always look exciting.

The reason for the relative simplicity of the Cobra is that Carroll Shelby was underfinanced when he started the project. At the beginning of the Sixties he was a successful race driver but he had a bad heart condition that precluded any more racing. Bringing his entrepreneurial instincts to bear, he went to AC Cars Ltd in England, which was then building a rather handsome sports car on a simple tubular frame using transverse leaf springs at each end. Shelby felt that this car would accept Ford's 260-cu-in. engine and be a marketable proposition. Prototypes were built and an order for 100 cars was placed, which were delivered early in 1963. Actually, only the first 75 cars had the 260-cu-in. engine because, at that time, Ford introduced the 289-cu-in. model that was offered in a high performance version putting out 271 bhp.

By now Ford was very interested in Shelby's project and the resulting racing successes. So, it was decided to redesign the car to take Ford's 427-cu-in. engine. Keeping things simple, the redesigning consisted mainly of using larger-diameter frame tubing and modernizing the suspension by using unequal-length A-arms with coil springs front and rear. The result was absolutely stunning in both performance and appearance. To accommodate the additional machinery, the car had to put on some fat so it is a much chunkier-looking car than the earlier 289; however, it is no more difficult to reproduce in fiberglass. Actually, it's a most interesting body because it was copied unashamedly in 1950 by English designer John Tojeiro from a Touring-bodied Ferrari 166 Mille Miglia.

For these reasons, the 427 Cobra is a relatively simple car to

PHOTOS BY JOHN LAMM

*Replica by Contemporary Classic.*

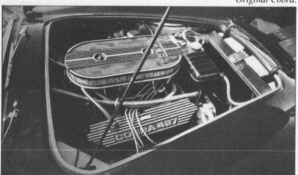

*Original Cobra.*

*Original Cobra.*

*Replica by ERA.*

*Replica by ERA.*

*Replica by Contemporary Classic.*

*Replica by Contemporary Classic.*

ROAD & TRACK

build today and its uncluttered fiberglass body doesn't present too many problems to anyone who has worked around boat-yards. Furthermore, the car's mechanical components are not too hard to find and the knowledge, skill and experience required are a lot less than those required for building, say, a replica of a Type 35 Bugatti. In fact, it is virtually impossible to tell a replica Cobra from an original.

When we arrived at Riverside Raceway, we found one or two people had brought their buddies along so we ended up with five cars, including one 289, and it was interesting to learn that four of them had been driven considerable distances to the track. The exception was the Contemporary which, having set wheel to ground only a few days before, was a bit of an unknown quantity and consequently arrived on a trailer. Unfortunately, it was also lacking a hood because the height of the intake manifold precluded the use of the normal panel and there had not been time to fabricate another one.

When I first asked Shelby what his feelings were about people building replicas of Cobras, he replied that he couldn't understand why the hell anyone would want to build a replica of a car that was already 20 years old when he built it. An interesting observation, but I suspect he is flattered and, although he doesn't knock replicas in any way, he does doubt the financial situation of some of the manufacturers. Once we had gotten ourselves all fired up and ready to go, the answer to my question to Shelby about replicas became obvious if for no other reason than that the cars were blindingly fast but handled, stopped, steered and behaved generally very well provided one paid due respect to the available power. Having a 427 myself, I recall writing a piece about Cobras for R&T in the July 1974 issue in which I said, "The Cobra is nothing more than a weapon designed specifically for proceeding from one point to another in the minimum amount of time."

Getting maximum-speed times for a very fast car at Riverside is difficult because the main straight has a sharp dogleg which can get a bit scary, and then there is the problem of asking the owner of a fast and extremely valuable car to let you belt the hell out of it. In addition, getting the most out of cars such as these requires a little practice.

The original 427, which was very kindly provided by Ron McClure, proved to be the fastest. It did 0–60 mph in 4.8 seconds and the ¼-mile in 13.3 sec with a terminal speed of 107.0 mph. The ERA, which was the factory demonstrator, did 0–60 mph in 5.6 sec and the quarter in 13.9 at 101.7 mph. From 0–100 mph, the original car took 11.3 sec compared to the ERA's 13.2 sec. Unfortunately, we were unable to get reliable figures on the Contemporary because it developed a bad wheel balance problem at higher speeds.

However, some months ago we had been able to drive the Contemporary demonstrator car and got some figures at a different location and under different conditions. That car did the quarter in about 13.5 sec at approximately 105.5 mph. These figures compare favorably with the figures we published in July 1974 for my own car, which showed the quarter at 13.8 sec with a terminal speed of 106.0 mph. Incidentally the 289 Cobra we tested in June 1964 was no slouch either because it did the quarter-mile in 14.0 sec with a terminal speed of 99.5 mph.

The major difference between the Contemporary and the ERA is that the ERA's frame tubes are rectangular but the Contemporary has round frame tubes as had the original cars. Both replicas use Jaguar independent suspension in the rear and the Contemporary uses E-Type Jag suspension in front. Because the rear suspension was used on the sedans as well as the sports cars, it is a relatively easy unit to obtain. Unfortunately, the E-Type front suspension was unique to that model and therefore rarer and more expensive. ERA, on the other hand, uses current Ford independent front suspension components.

With regard to the engines, there is a certain amount of confusion. The original 427s came equipped with racing 427 engines that were side-oilers and had cross-bolted main bearings. However, the supply of true 427s was limited and 428s were sometimes used instead. In fact, the two engines were used somewhat randomly so one batch of cars would have 427s and another batch might have 428s. The 428 was a totally different engine and was used to power the bigger models in the Ford and Lincoln-Mercury lines. However, as Carroll Shelby says, how do you tell the difference between 425 bhp and 475 bhp? Comparing the two engines, Shelby says that the 428 is a bit quicker at the bottom end of the range but the 427 starts to build up at the top end. In addition, Shelby told me that the 427 would occasionally throw a rod for no particular reason when you were cruising along at 3000 rpm. Fortunately, I'm glad to say, this has not been my experience.

Obtaining a suitable transmission to handle the power of a 427 or 428 engine is no particular problem because plenty of the original Ford top-loaders are available, and it's a beautiful transmission, well able to handle the highest torque outputs. Alternatively, you can get a Doug Nash 5-speed, although the gears in the original gearbox are so well spaced for such a torquey engine that five are not really necessary. For those people who don't like to shift, Ford's C6 automatic does the job nicely.

One of the greatest advantges of buying a replica, particularly if you have sufficient mechanical skill to buy it in kit form and assemble it yourself, is that you can tailor the car to your own particular desires and requirements. For instance, the original 427 engines came with a compression ratio of 11.5:1, but that was in the days when you could buy gasoline that was in excess of 100 octane at almost any gas station. Today, that kind of compression ratio would require either avgas or a big and expensive dose of some sort of additive. Therefore, the answer is to go to a much lower ratio. Actually, the power-to-weight ratio of a Cobra is such that almost any V-8, used or new, would give the car pretty sensational performance.

Just because you are buying a Cobra replica doesn't mean that you have to have a 427 or 428 engine. The Ford 351 Cleveland engine makes a good power unit for the car and can be obtained in various stages of tune. One reason for not electing to use a true 427 is that it will probably cost you a good $3000 from a reputable engine rebuilder. In addition, there are many Chevrolet enthusiasts around and quite a few of the Cobra replicas are Chevy-powered.

ERA and Contemporary have somewhat different methods of marketing their products. ERA prefers to sell one kit for $14,800 that is a bolt-together design with no fabricating at all. What you get is a complete body and chassis with all instruments, cooling system, fuel system, electrical system, windshield, bumpers, etc, and these are either already installed or ready for installation when the running gear has been obtained. Also included in the kit is a list of part numbers and sources for various minor items such as radiator hoses, fan belts and other pieces that will depend on the type of power unit used. What you have to provide are the engine, transmission, Jaguar final drive/rear suspension unit, Datsun Z-car rack and pinion, Triumph Spitfire steering column, Chevrolet Camaro disc brakes, front coil over shock units, steering wheel, road wheels and tires and MGB windshield wiper motor.

On the other hand, Contemporary offers three different kits ranging from a body/frame unit at $6750 to a package similar to ERA's at $13,450 and, in between, a basic home-builder package at $8150. Also, any of the three packages can be had with

totally rebuilt and assembled suspension and brakes for an additional $4250. Depending on the depth of your pocket and your available time and skill, you could complete a Cobra replica for about $20,000, but for those who are busy and not so adept, the best way is to buy the most comprehensive kit.

Both ERA and Contemporary claim that virtually all the kits they have sold have either been completed or are being worked on actively. This is because most of the customers are true enthusiasts who have always wanted something like a Cobra but have never been able to afford one.

Our time spent at Riverside was unfortunately all too short. Carroll Shelby enjoyed himself immensely, perhaps because although he owns one of each of the various Cobra models, he doesn't drive them much, preferring to dash around the back roads of Texas on a fast motorcycle. His general opinion of the replicas was that they were just as quick as the originals but they had softer suspensions; for really fast driving over varying conditions, an original would be a bit quicker. On the other hand, he felt the replicas were ideal for everyday road driving.

What we learned at Riverside, and I knew from owning one, is that you have to treat a Cobra with respect and it doesn't matter whether it's an original or a replica. With a weight of something over 2500 lb and perhaps 450 bhp available, depending on the engine, you have a power-to-weight ratio that is something fierce.

Perhaps one can sum up the 427 Cobra by saying that the late Ken Miles, who was a Cobra driver and developer, once took one of the cars from 0–100 mph and back down to a complete stop in 13.8 sec. With $20,000 and some knowledge and skill, perhaps you could go out and do likewise. ⓦ

PHOTO BY JOE RUSZ

PHOTOS BY RICHARD M. BARON

# THE CANADIAN COBRA

TOTALLY DIFFERENT IN concept to the ERA and Contemporary Classic Cobras is the Aurora made by Aurora cars of Richmond Hill, Ontario, Canada. This replica can only be bought as a complete car. However, it is equally desirable to the less mechanically adept enthusiast. Furthermore, it is a replica of the earlier 289 version of the Cobra, which some people prefer to the more chunky 427.

It meets all emissions and safety regu-

lations and carries a warranty of six months or 10,000 miles. Obviously it caters to a totally different market and when I talked to the Aurora folks they said their average buyer was between 35 and 50 and was fulfilling his dream of owning a sports car totally different from anything else on his block. Put in its proper context, the car meets these requirements very well indeed. What it is, in fact, is a modern high performance sports car clothed with a Cobra body, and there

is absolutely nothing wrong in that.

When Carroll Shelby first went to work on the 289 Cobra, it was even then somewhat archaic. To attempt to re-create the 289 two decades later would obviously be a mistake and so there is virtually nothing in the Aurora that even resembles the 289 except the body, which is an exact replica.

Aurora builds its own tubular frame and then relies on Ford for some of the components. The engine is the stock Ford 302-cu-in. V-8 and it is mated to either Ford's 4-speed manual transmission or to an automatic. The suspension is fully independent and the brakes are 10.0-in. solid discs mounted inboard at the rear and 9.5-in. ventilated discs in front. Steering is by rack and pinion and the standard tires are Michelin TRX with Pirelli Cinturatos as an option. The finish is very good, with the fiberglass panels being made by C&C Yachts, which has an excellent reputation in the yachting world, and the interior is done in real leather. Unfortunately, the best things in life are not free and the Aurora comes out at $36,000.

On the road, the car inspired confidence, particularly in braking and steering, and we couldn't quibble about the roadholding either. Out at the track, we managed to get a ¼-mile time of 14.9 sec and a terminal speed of 91.0 mph, while 0–100 mph came up in 18.8 sec.

Although these times and speeds are no where near those of the 427 Cobras, they are still impressive. With this kind of performance in a well designed car using many stock components, mostly of Ford origin, the Aurora provides a good alternative for someone who wants a Cobra replica but lacks either the time or the mechanical knowledge to assemble a kit.—*Tony Hogg*